THE REAL
DAD'S ARMY

The Story of the Home Guard

NORMAN LONGMATE

AMBERLEY

This edition first published 2012

Amberley Publishing
The Hill, Stroud
Gloucestershire, GL5 4EP

www.amberley-books.com

British Library Cataloguing in Publication Data.
A catalogue record for this book is available from the British Library.

ISBN 978-1-4456-0688-0

Typesetting and Origination by Amberley Publishing.
Printed in Great Britain.

THE REAL
DAD'S
ARMY

About the Author

NORMAN LONGMATE, ex-Private 'F' Company, 3rd Sussex Battalion, Home Guard, joined 'Dad's Army' at the same age as the fictional character 'Pike', seventeen. To this day he contends that the much-loved sitcom was remarkably accurate in it's portrayal of life in the Home Guard. After the war he read modern history at Worcester College, Oxford and went on to work as a journalist and radio producer of history documentaries. He is a Fellow of the Royal Historical Society and has written more than thirty books, mainly on the Second World War. For this book, and many others, he made requests through regional newspapers for veterans to contact him with their memories. He was historical adviser on the hugely popular Channel 4 TV show, *The 1940 House*. He lives in London.

Praise for Norman Longmate

Doodlebugs: The Story of the Flying Bombs
'Consolidates his position as the most evocative historian of the 1940s Home Front' *THE TIMES*
'Full of sad, funny and harrowing anecdotes'
THE DAILY TELEGRAPH

How We Lived Then: A History of Everyday Life During the Second World War
'Minutely detailed, accurate, skillfully marshalled and engagingly written'
THE SPECTATOR
'A marvelously comprehensive panorama of the six shattering years, misses nothing' *THE SUNDAY TELEGRAPH*

Island Fortress
'An enthralling account' JAN MORRIS, *THE INDEPENDENT*
'Elegantly written, constantly fascinating, narrative history at its best' *THE GUARDIAN*

Air Raid: Coventry 1940
'The definitive account' *COVENTRY EVENING CHRONICLE*

The Home Front
'A wonderful book' JENNY UGLOW

CONTENTS

I
Give Them LDV!

The first day I got my uniform... the missus looked at me and she said. 'What are you supposed to be?' I said, 'I'm one of the Home Guards.' She said, 'What are you supposed to do?' I said, 'Supposed to do, I' supposed to stop Hitler's army landing.' She said 'What, YOU?' I said 'No, not me, there's Billy Brightside, Charlie Evans and Joe Battersby, there's seven or eight of us.... We're on guard on a little hut behind the Dog and Pullet.' She said, 'I suppose that was your idea?' I said, 'Yes, and that Charlie Evans wants to claim it as his.'

ROBB WILTON in radio sketch, 'The Day I Joined the Home Guard'

It began, like the war itself, with a broadcast. On the evening of Tuesday 14 May 1940 the newly-appointed Secretary of State for

War, Anthony Eden, appeared on the BBC Home Service. Four days earlier, on the previous Friday, the Germans had begun their long-awaited offensive in the West and already alarming reports of their success, and the unexpected methods they had used to achieve it, were reaching Britain, as Eden explained:

I want to speak to you tonight about the form of warfare which the Germans have been employing so extensively against Holland and Belgium — namely the dropping of parachute troops behind the main defensive lines.... In order to leave nothing to chance, and to supplement from sources as yet untapped the means of defence already arranged, we are going to ask you to help us in a manner which I know will be welcome to thousands of you. Since the war began the government have received countless enquiries from all over the kingdom from men of all ages who are for one reason or another not at present engaged in military service, and who wish to do something for the defence of their country. Well, now is your opportunity.

We want large numbers of such men in Great Britain, who are British subjects, between the ages of seventeen and sixty-five...
to come forward and offer their services.... The name of the new force which is now to be raised will be 'The Local Defence Volunteers'.... This name describes its duties in three words... This is... a part-time job , so there will be no need for any volunteer to abandon his present occupation.... When on duty you will form part of the armed forces.... You will not be paid, but you will receive a uniform and be armed.... In order to volunteer, what you have to do is give in your name at your local police station; and then, as and when we want you, we will let you know.

1. Scarborough volunteers demonstrate their readiness, June 1940.

THE FIRST PARADE!

2. The first parade of the ramshackle LDV. From *Home Guard Humour*, 1944.

And so, in between the 9 o'clock news and a documentary programme 'The Voice of the Nazi' on the BBC, was launched the largest, strangest and — if the truth be told — least military volunteer army in Britain's long history. For the War Minister had been right. Not thousands but hundreds of thousands of men were not merely willing but eager to 'have a crack' at Hitler, whom most people in Britain regarded by now not only as the leader of Germany but as a personal enemy.

The rush to the colours began at once. One York housewife remembers her husband going out without a word. Jumping on his motorcycle and roaring off two miles to the police station. But quick as he had been another man was there before him. At many other places the first applicants were round at the police station before Eden had finished speaking. The flood continued next morning, although the police were not always very welcoming, as the novelist Ernest Raymond, who had served in Gallipoli as an Army padre and was now an air raid warden at Haywards Heath in Sussex, discovered:

Enthusiastically resolved to be transformed from a civilian warden to a combatant of sorts I was at our police station after breakfast next morning. I confess I expected some praise for this promptitude, as I passed through the sandbag barrier that protected the station's doorway. It was not forthcoming. The uniformed policeman behind the desk sighed as he said, 'We can take your name and address. That's all.' A detective-inspector in mufti, whom I knew, explained this absence of fervour. 'You're about the hundred-and-fiftieth who's come in so far, Mr Raymond, and it's not yet half past nine. Ten per cent of 'em may be of some use to Mr Eden but, lor' luv-a-duck, we've had 'em stumping in more or less on crutches. We've taken

3. A Local Defence Volunteer.

their names but this is going to be Alexander's rag-time army.'

As I passed out through the sandbags I met three more volunteers about to file in through the crack. I knew them all. One was an elderly gentleman-farmer who'd brought his sporting gun...
Another had his hunting dog with him;.... All explained that they were 'joining up'... so I prepared them for the worst, I said, 'Well, don't expect any welcome in there. They don't love us. And get it over quickly. I rather suspected that if I stayed around too long, I'd be arrested for loitering.'

Everywhere the response was overwhelming. This was the experience of one ex-officer who had taken on the job of enrolling applicants at Canterbury Road Police Station in Perry Bar, Birmingham:

The weather was sweltering and we were allotted the small decontamination room in the police station yard.... Applicants seemed to form a never-ending stream. They started to queue up as soon as they could leave their work and by 11 p.m. there were still scores of them waiting to enrol. Every night we worked until the small hours of the morning, trying to get some sort of shape into the organisation in preparation for the next day's rush. Within a few days the platoon was three or four hundred strong and it seemed that if every police station were experiencing the same influx, all the male population in Birmingham would be enrolled within a week or two.

Over the country as a whole 250,000 men, equal in numbers to the peacetime Regular Army, gave in their names in the first twenty-four hours. The supply of enrolment forms soon proved inadequate. In Bideford, in Devon, where 240 volunteers had been expected and 1046 were to sign on by 1 August, a local resident and future LDV commander, filled the gap by commissioning a local printer to copy the official form. Many enrolment forms were run off on an office duplicator or recruits signed a temporary slip promising to fill in the proper document when they got the chance. As the news grew worse, the desire to serve increased. On 17 June France surrendered and Britain stood alone. By the end of that month volunteers for the LDV numbered nearly one and a half million, not far short of the Army's wartime strengths, conscripts and all.

Many people had, even before mid-May, suggested the formation of a force of armed civilians. As early as March one titled lady living in style near Ross-on-Wye had, like a medieval baron, formed her domestic staff and tenants into the 'Much Marcle Watchers', who kept a vigilant eye open for any parachutists daring to descend on her estates. She had even optimistically, though unsuccessfully, asked the local Army commander for eight rifles 'with a couple of machine guns if you have any'. But the LDV really began with a meeting at the War Office on 11 May. There was no red tape because there was no time to introduce it, though some Civil Servants did their best. One early draft of the proposed enrolment form contained seventeen questions and twelve sub-questions, among them such enquiries as: 'Are you willing to be vaccinated?'

The government would have preferred to wait till an organisation had been set up to deal with them before appealing for volunteers for the new force, but with the situation in France growing worse every hour there was no time. The LDV was launched without any staff, or funds or premises of its own. To organise those who came forward into units and to get the LDV 'off the ground' the War Office relied on public-spirited people, preferably retired officers, living locally, who would, it was hoped, take over command at first and look through the lists of volunteers for suitable 'officers' and 'NCO's'. The idea was to choose the most senior officers first, for them to select the next rank down, who would in turn choose their sub-ordinates. To start the whole process off telegrams were sent to the Lord Lieutenant of each county and to a much newer figure, the Regional Commissioner. There were twelve such Commissioners, each responsible for one of the Civil Defence Regions into which the British Isles were divided, with authority to become a temporary dictator in case of invasion.

The Lord Lieutenant was important for another reason. He was automatically president of the County Territorial Association, and the 'Terriers' possessed offices, drill halls and clerical staff. Unfortunately, its members having marched off to war a year earlier, the TA organisation in some places hardly existed, but the War Office hoped it could be revived and provide a ready-made machine through which the LDV could be supplied.

The Army was also expected to help but already had its hands full and at the start the LDV was pretty much on its own. Eventually, however, the plan was to link it to the Army through the seven Army Commands into which the British Isles (excluding Northern Ireland) were divided. Each command would now be sub-divided into LDV Areas, in turn broken down into Zones or Groups (according to population). Below these came the battalions. A battalion consisted of four companies, each made up of four platoons which normally contained three sections. Unlike Army units, those in the LDV had no fixed 'establishment'. A battalion could vary in strength from as few as 640 men to as many as 1600,

4. & 5. Many of the running jokes in the BBC TV series *Dad's Army* were not new. From *Home Guard Humour*, 1944.

ISSUING BATTLE DRESS

though most were somewhere around 1000 strong.

At first many hardly knew what platoon they belonged to, let alone what battalion, and empire-building commanders were able to 'poach' whole Sections from their less wide-awake neighbours. But everyone was clear enough who the enemy was and in the areas of South East and Eastern England most immediately threatened some astonishing feats of improvisation were achieved in getting men out on patrol within hours of their coming forward. In most places it was not for at least another week or two that any appreciable number of LDVs were standing to.

One man who was present at the meeting at St Columb found that 'a crowd representing a good cross-section of the community filled the large open-air cattle market', for car-owners all over the area had filled their cars with passengers and brought them to the meeting. 'Brief addresses were given by two speakers, many questions were asked and answered... everyone was anxious to get down to work.' Next evening the Magwan Porth contingent met at the local café, voted a popular local farmer into the chair and 'patrol areas were marked out from Watergate Bay Hotel to the bridge at Mawgan Porth... from the bridge to the Tea House at Bedruthan', the first patrols setting off the same evening.

At Wilmington in Sussex a platoon had been formed, after a meeting at the village pub:

A day or two later the vet, who had been a major in Egypt in the last war, told us he had been asked to enrol volunteers from ours and neighbouring villages.

Well, this being a democracy, the chaps decided we had better talk it over. A meeting was arranged at the village pub, the *Black*

Horse. The boss there (since killed bombing Germany) and I commandeered a car to tour the district and rope people in. The car was a small Ford belonging to a villager who had jacked it up for the duration. He had removed the battery.... Mine host from the pub was a bit of an electrician, and he scrounged a second-hand battery from a friend's garage at Polegate and we soon had the car going. We really had no right to pinch that car, and it wasn't insured anyhow, but the owner was a good old sort who didn't mind.

Everywhere now similar meetings were being held. At Cambridge the first volunteers assembled in the somewhat gruesome surroundings of the School of Anatomy; while a Middlesex Company, which liked to describe itself as defending the 'North West (London) Frontier', started life at a suburban tea party as one member recorded:

I gladly accepted, hoping that I would be served out with rifle and ammunition and I was surprised — not to say irritated — to find, on arrival, more of the atmosphere of an 'At Home' than a meeting of soldiers preparing to face at any moment a merciless and ruthless enemy. There were introductions, followed by some talk.... I waited for some warlike move to be made in that sunny, comfortable sitting room.... The next happening was the arrival of tea; but not tea alone; cakes and strawberries and cream were also handed round.

One difficulty that soon became obvious was that potential leaders were not distributed evenly throughout the country. In favoured retirement areas like Cheltenham or Bournemouth one could have formed whole companies out of ex-majors and colonels; in some East End boroughs it was hard to discover a single former lieutenant. In Chelsea there was a fine concentration of former 'top brass', including General Sir Hubert Gough, who had been in command of a whole Army in France in 1918 but now found it hard to join up as an ordinary private. After the usual rush of volunteers, 'for some weeks', he later wrote, 'no-one in Chelsea heard anything further... Chelsea Town Hall was bombarded with eager but indignant enquirers' and at last, in despair of higher authority helping, the Town Clerk asked Sir Hubert to get things moving. It proved no easy task. The police at first refused to part with the vital list of names and addresses of volunteers, which he only obtained after appealing direct to a very senior officer indeed, and this proved only the first skirmish in a long battle:

...We began drill, usually in the gardens of the various squares, but the next shock we received was to be told that we were merely to reinforce the police and keep order.... It was even suggested that the only useful function we could perform would be to march in bodies of fifty or more, armed with batons, through the streets at moments of crisis in order to give moral support to the terrified population by our martial bearing. The officers and men were furious and the police made it quite clear that they did not want us.

The LDV was treated from the first day by the Whitehall bureaucrats who drew up the detailed regulations and vetted the accounts with outstanding meanness so at the beginning almost everyone connected with the LDV was out of pocket. Many commanders set up headquarters in their own homes, bought typewriters, and engaged clerks, with their own money. Several headquarters had their telephones cut off by the Post Office for not

6. London recruiting march June 1940.

7. Railway employees mount guard along the track.

8. Lord Strabolgi and his fellow legislators train in the courtyard of St Stephens Palace.

paying the bill; in Cambridgeshire one battalion was told it could not train on Sunday unless it was prepared to pay overtime to the signalman who had to be on duty to open a gate for them.

But they most serious problem at first was finding premises. The Warwick Battalion which, as described earlier, had started life in the bare, uncomfortable Decontamination Room at the Canterbury Road Police Station, found that even there 'we were not exactly welcome and were, in fact, politely asked to leave. On doing so we took up our quarters in schoolrooms, using the playgrounds as and when we could, for exercises.... In a very few months we had used as our headquarters no fewer than three different schools', being forced to move 'by reason of their inadequate blackout.' Other units had the same trouble. Church halls, miners institutes, scout-huts and similar buildings were often lent at first but dual-occupation soon became irritating to both parties, and it was embarrassing and humiliating to have to postpone a weapon-training session to make way for the parish social or a tenderfoots' test. Once weapons began to arrive, finding a satisfactory room where they could be kept safe was even more important. The official answer, that they should be stored at the nearest Army camp, or deposited at the local police station, was not really practicable and most units made their own arrangements. An Edgware platoon, with six precious rifles between twenty men, hid them 'in a cupboard under the roof' in its improvised headquarters, 'from which they were extracted each night after much groping with a torch. To avoid this waste of valuable time a rifle rack was constructed... chained and secured with a combination padlock.... The rack eventually fell to pieces as a result of being dismembered each night by guard commanders who had forgotten the code.'

A Bristol unit believed all its troubles were over when the

commander was offered the use of the Territorials' premises, but things did not work out as he had expected:

Having completed our enrolment for the night, we now gathered our men into four companies and... very proudly the leading company marched into the local Territorial Army headquarters. The amazed sentry at the gate stared goggle-eyed at the orderly if ill-assorted crowd that marched past him, as he bawled for the Sergeant of the Guard. Suddenly a very amazed officer appeared.... He fired off a stream of remarks about the clothing, appearance and parenthood of our motley crew. When he had to some degree recovered his equilibrium, it was discovered that the headquarters had been a donation to us from someone who did not posses the power to give and, furthermore, the people who were actually in residence had no idea that they were to be assisted by so ready and able a contingent. Reluctantly, we therefore split into four companies, each company commander gathering up his unwanted sheep on to any piece of waste land or school yard that would hold them.

But at least this officer discovered, whatever the difficulties there was no lack of keenness among his men:

One morning, at about four a.m. I opened the door of the building and beheld a remarkable figure. Standing in the light, which streamed from the open doorway of the guardroom, was a crouching figure, full of expectant energy ready to spring, armed with a knobkerry as big as his little self. A large cap with an enormous peak (was) pulled over his right eye, a tremendous and not too clean muffler about his neck, a jacket that reached nearly to his knees and trousers with many turn-ups at the ankles and much frayed at the same place. There he stood with a villainous leer, the complete picture of hate and ferocity. 'Who's there?', he growled, in a voice calculated to send shivers down the back of even a brave man. As I emerged from the darkness into the light of the doorway, a wonderful change took place. This foul and evil thing was suddenly jerked into a smiling and very confused boy who said he was eighteen. In his confusion, he attempted to salute. Forgetting he still held his enormous weapon in his right hand, he dealt himself a resounding wallop on the head, which sent his vile cap flying in the dust and laid him apparently lifeless at my feet.

The official upper age limit of sixty-five was not at first enforced. The earliest MP to sign on admitted to being sixty-eight and one unit boasted that its officer had been personally nursed by Florence Nightingale in the Crimea — thought this seems unlikely, as it would have made him at least 104. Generally accepted as the oldest LDV was an ex-company Sergeant Major in the Black Watch, Alexander Taylor, of Creiff in Scotland, who had served in the Sudan campaign of 1885, as well as in South Africa and Flanders. On joining up in 1940 he was asked no awkward questions about his age but 'simply handed... a pitchfork from the armoury and detailed... to join the section guarding the gasworks'. He was still serving on his eightieth birthday (by special dispensation of the War Office) and was presented on parade with an ornamental clock, a ceremony probably unique in British military history. 'There is no truth in the rumour that our old friend, Private Taylor, fought at Bannockburn', remarked the company commander making the presentation, 'but... he has fought in practically every damn battle since.'

9. LDV men practice at Bisley.

10. London park keepers swing into training.

The government had at first thought of confining the LDV to ex-servicemen and, as they had hoped, they made up a large proportion of the first intake. Almost all the earliest officers had served before, many as professional soldiers. Some found it hard to adjust to the idea of a basically civilian army. In one Devon village there was actually a fight between an 'elderly retired Army captain', entrusted with forming a local unit, who 'roped in his pals of like kind' and one 'young man who asked why *he* hadn't been invited to join' and was insultingly informed that he didn't measure up to the required social standards. Undoubtedly being back in uniform again, went to some elderly officers' heads and one, in London, even introduced a 'dining in night' for his officers in an impromptu mess when, instead of getting on with much-needed training, they assembled in black bow-ties and denim uniforms to pass the port.

Military experience was at first rated more important that physical fitness. The official requirement was that any recruit 'must be capable of free movement', but nothing was laid down about how far or how fast. Later, standards were considerably tightened up and the visibly infirm persuaded to resign. Being free to leave when one liked was one, much prized, way in which the LDV differed from any other army. All that was required was to give a fortnight's notice under what was nicknamed 'the housemaid's clause'. Unsatisfactory recruits could also be got rid of under the classic formula 'services no longer required', no reason being given. Strictly speaking an LDV while on duty was subject to military law, but every effort was made to avoid wasting time on courts-martial, and during the whole war there were very few indeed. Wherever possible, offenders were charged with civil offences, the first probably being a Liverpool LDV fined £10 for being drunk in charge of a rifle. Civilians who refused to obey LDV orders were also handed over to the police; there was great satisfaction in LDV ranks when one bank clerk, who told a sentry that his name was Tom Mix (a famous cowboy film star) and refused to produce his identity card, was sent to jail for fourteen days.

Inevitably a few misfits were recruited at first, but they usually dropped out fairly soon after serious training began. One stalwart farmer in Lancashire insisted that, having once killed a mad bull with his first shot, he required no military training of any kind. Another elderly recruit in the same battalion was prepared to sit behind a hedge and shoot at any German who came along but not attend parades or exercises, and when told his commander had other ideas retorted: 'You'd better scratch me off.' Another individualist, a Somerset farmer's son, did not take kindly to drill and firmly refused to move his left foot into line with his right, replying to all pleas and orders: 'It be good enough for I.' He, too, did not last long.

But for every man who dropped out there were half a dozen new volunteers, until a ban had to be put on accepting more recruits until those already enrolled had been absorbed. Many men, having joined up themselves, did their best to bring in additional members; golf clubs, containing many retired officers, being a particularly fertile recruiting ground. At the Cobble Hall Club, near Leeds, fifty-seven golfers (of whom eighteen were ex-officers) and several ex-servicemen, formed a self-contained platoon which took over the defence of their course against the intrusion of any German non-members who might arrive without paying the usual green fee. The unit's first Standing Orders for patrols had a distinctive flavour:

Dress: Golf gear

Arms: A stout stick
Guardroom: Club lounge — easy chairs for sleep

At first, too, 'reports had a smack of golf in them, for example: "Flares seen over the 13th green. Flashing light at 105 degrees from the 7th tee".' Membership proved to be popular and four-man patrols would play a round of golf together before setting off for work.

Huntsmen who knew the countryside were also much prized as recruits. Among those who joined up in Hertfordshire was the tenth Earl of Cavan, Master of Foxhounds, who arrived to offer the services of himself, and his horse, as a despatch rider, while his chauffeur signed on at the same time, with the Earl's car. The Earl, a former field marshal who had served in campaigns in every corner of the globe, was soon occupying a humble position, as NCO in charge of the Headquarters Communication Platoon.

Government departments, perhaps sensitive to jokes about chairborne warriors, proved a fruitful source of LDVs. Few had such a hard time as those posted, in civilian suits and steel helmets, at the entrance to the War Office, who were subjected to a critical inspection by every Brass Hat who passed. The Ministry of Food formed its own company and ultimately its own battalion, though its units had at first names somewhat reminiscent of the Quartermaster's Stores. The Bacon and Ham Division of the Ministry (responsible for safeguarding the nation's ration of four ounces of one or the other, but not both) mustered sixty-two men for Lord Woolton's first inspection, the Sugar and Starch Division (eight ounces of sugar per ration book, unlimited starch) twenty-four. This turnout was not wholly due to patriotism, strong hints being dropped that the authorities would smile on any man who

11. Maidenhead factory workers training during their midday breaks.

12. Home Guard train in the correct use of the bayonet.

volunteered. But such pressure was exceptional and sometimes, without urging, the whole staff of a department or office signed on.

Many private employers also formed their own units for every firm or factory wanted to show publicly its determination to stand firm, and how better to do so than putting its men into uniform and giving them arms? There, of course was the rub: in the early weeks the LDV rarely had either. As German radio demanded: 'Under *what* arms? Broomsticks, or the arms of the local pub, with pots of beer and darts in their hands?' More serious was the official warning from the German government that 'civilians who take up arms against German soldiers are... no better than murderers, whether they are priests or bank clerks'.

The LDVs only hope — a faint one — of escaping a German firing squad lay in being visibly in military uniform. The LDVs uniform, according to Sir Edward Grigg, Eden's deputy and the minister principally responsible for the LDV, consisted of 'civilian clothes with khaki armbands stitched to the sleeve, having the letters "LDV" stencilled in white'. Following its usual practice of giving humble objects imposing names the Army described this strip of cloth as a 'brassard', and one Berkshire unit, peacefully patrolling the grounds of Radley College that summer, decided there was perhaps something to be said for doing so. After an urgent message arrived that 'an armed band was at Chestnut Avenue... reserves were summoned and a strong patrol hurried off into the darkness, expecting to meet a sticky end' only to discover on arrival that all the caller had said was that they wanted 'arm bands'. But at first even this three-inch wide strip of canvas was lacking, though in some places members of the Women's Voluntary Services rallied round to manufacture them with the help of a homemade stencil.

13. LDV practise shooting down German parachutist using a teddy bear..

14. Home Guards were often first on the scene when enemy aircraft crashed.

the commander of one Buckinghamshire battalion made the supreme sacrifice and handed over his old First World War puttees to be cut up. (How the LDV became a uniformed force is described in a later chapter.) The first landmark in the LDV's history was the announcement by Sir Edward Grigg on 22 May that a quarter of a million armbands were on the way. This seems to have been the occasion, too, of the first public joke at the new force's expense. Instead of issuing armbands, suggested one MP, why not have the letters LDV tattooed on each volunteer's arm?

airborne troops *had* been used, but in normal military units and only to capture key forts and secure bridgeheads in advance of the attacking armies. The Germans were soon to plan the invasion of the British Isles in the same way: the hordes of parachutists for whom the LDVs so diligently scanned the skies never existed.

On 22 May, a week after the LDV's formation, with the British Expeditionary Force already in full retreat towards Dunkirk, the Under-Secretary of State for War set out 'the three main purposes for which the Local Defence Volunteers are wanted':

First, observation and information. We want the earliest possible information, either from observation posts or from patrols as to landings. the second purpose is to help, in the very earliest stages, or preventing movement by these enemy parties landed from the air, by blocking roads... so that they are hemmed in... from the moment they land. Their third purpose is to assist in patrolling and protecting vulnerable spots, of which there is a great number everywhere.

he first need, at least outside the towns, was for an OP, as ery true LDV soon learned to call an Observation Post, though erans of the First World War tended to refer to it as an 'O Pip', Ernest Raymond, in Sussex:

e church of our small town stood on a hill, and its square tower, ugh squat, commanded from its top a spacious view of the atry around. No better 'O Pip'... than this and... my section responsible for it....

ie evening watch was 9.30 to 1.30, the dawn watch from :o 5.30.... One of my section was... Christopher Stone, most

2
From Dusk To Dawn

In the event of observing German parachutists landing, telephone High Wycombe 26.

Standing orders of 4th Battalion, Buckinghamshire LDV, Summer 1940.

One commander later described the first hectic, heroic weeks of the LDVs existence as the 'haphazard period' of its life. This it certainly was; but it was also a cheerful, informal time, and in the air, too there was an intense patriotism, as recalled by one ex-officer in a Cornish company after night-duty at the end of May:

And so with frequent calls at the hotel for refreshment, the long night passed and the sun came up on yet another Monday. But there was a subtle difference between this Monday and those that had gone before. We had our backs to the wall but, God willing, we would fight to the last to preserve our country and all we held sacred and dear.

This same determination to sell one's life dearly if the Germans came, but not to be too uncomfortable while waiting, was revealed by another member of the same unit, who arrived on watch 'equipped with an umbrella and hurricane lamp and armed to the teeth with a pasty'.

The duties of the LDV at this stage, as one retired major wrote, 'were summed up correctly in three words "Observation and Report". If an enemy arrived on the scene it was the job of the patrol or post to keep him under observation and, by hook or by crook, get the information by telephone or messenger to the Police HQ. After this had been done, other contacts must be made, but there must be no misunderstanding as to which came first. At this period many a Volunteer, having delivered his message, would have "sat back" in confident expectation of the speedy arrival of regular troops conducted by the local constable.'

The nickname, the 'Look, Duck and Vanish' brigade, which some members of the LDV gave to it, reflected their true purpose very well — certainly better than such humorous alternatives as the Long Dentured Veterans or Last Desperate Venture. The name coined by the popular press, 'parashots', never caught on, and was in any case misleading; most LDVs could not at this stage have greeted an enemy paratrooper with anything more lethal than a pitchfork.

We now know the whole parachutist scare was founded on a massive misconception. France had been beaten by conventional, uniformed, land forces, superbly trained and handled. Some

15. An evening route march takes the local Home Guard unit through the village high

16. Local Defence Volunteers prepare for the real thing. LDV p
barricades against invading German troops.

celebrated of the early disc-jockeys. I used to like having him as my mate on the tower for a night watch, since he always arrive with a camp chair and a hamper, packed with chicken and salad and sandwiches and cakes and bottles of wine — on a good night champagne.... I remember tracts of the long night under the stars — never any rain that wonderful summer — when, instead of being behind my binoculars and sweeping the broad landscape for parachutists, I was guiltily seated, shaking with laughter at his stories as I drank his wine or shared his chicken, while the rolling green fields of Sussex lay open to the enemy. One householder near the church complained that our voices and laughter kept him awake... I was instructed that this manner of laughing up there 'must cease forthwith'.

Climbing a hundred or more steps exhausted some elderly LDVs, whose doctors had instructed them never to use ladders, and sometimes the clergy were persuaded to undertake these vigils for them. In a Lancashire town all the clergy shared out the duty of watching twice a week, which provided the occasion for many a vigorous inter-denominational discussion. The fiancée of one curate felt, however, that his most heroic action was in helping the police to direct the traffic while dressed in khaki uniform and clerical collar, which, she reflects 'didn't do much good because a crowd used to collect to watch'.

Where no conveniently placed church tower existed, units found the best shelter they could. Old cars were popular, but attracted destructive children — the curse of many LDV units — and tended to be too comfortable: younger sentries were often found asleep on the back seat. The Wilmington, Sussex, platoon, whose formation was described in the last chapter, met this need as resourcefully as it did every other:

Our chief observation post was an exposed hilltop, which meant a long walk from the village and a stiff climb at the end. It was all right in the summer, but we felt we should need shelter in the bleak winter. So a deputation went to a gypsy encampment and bargained for an old caravan. We got it for, I think, under 5 pounds, using the funds subscribed in the village. We spent a bit more money on paint for camouflage, which to my mind made the gypsy caravan more conspicuous than ever after our amateur efforts. A farmer lent us a horse to fetch it. We had about five miles to go. Then at the village we borrowed another horse, and with the help of about half a dozen of the squad, and the village women and children cheering us as we sweated, we pulled, pushed and shoved the broken-down caravan right to the top of the Downs. That job took hours. We were nearly driven crazy by bugs in the caravan but I still have sentimental memories of the old home, and of the acceptable comfort it gave us on windy nights when the planes were zooming over out heads. Sometimes there was competition for the night turn, and the men would chivvy each other about wanting an alibi for the wife for a night off.

The vermin from which the men suffered there were no doubt as unpopular with their wives as they were with LDVs, for many husbands now bought home with them unwanted companions of this kind, acquired in some unsavoury overnight Observation Point or guardroom. While the LDV prepared to fight the Germans, their families waged an equally remorseless but more immediate battle against other invaders with Flit and Keatings Powder.

Men stood guard that summer and autumn in a strange variety

THE MOBILE SECTION !

17. Improvised transport. From *Home Guard Humour*, 1944.

18. This tower, on the estate of Lord Hastings, has once again come into its own. Used during five previous threats of invasion, it serves today as a Home Guard observation post.

of places. A Hampstead platoon shared 'Queen Mary's Maternity Home at the top of Heath Street', vacated by its normal residents, with the fire service. The Ministry of Food volunteers sent a detachment each night to the local railway station, Colwyn Bay, which normally had little traffic, and occupied the waiting room, but 'frequently the 8.50 or the 9.40 p.m. would appear at anything from 2 to 5 a.m. and the guard would find themselves giving up their fires and palliasses to stranded wayfarers who could not reach their homes'. 'B' Platoon of No. 6 Company, 23rd Middlesex Battalion (whose origins over the strawberries and cream in Edgware have already been described) finding themselves shut out of the school assigned to them by a rival company, which simply refused to move, decided to build their own headquarters cum dugout on an abandoned housing estate which conveniently overlooked their main defensive line 'the railway cutting of the Canons Park to Stanmore Railway'.

The interior was equipped with wire netting bunks, a lamp and other refinements, and 'B' Platoon moved in to what must have been the most luxurious dugout in the country, which would not have disgraced the Front Line on the Western Front in 1918. It needed, however, constant 'maintenance works' due to 'the depredations of small boys'. Later the platoon decided to abandon this advanced post and retreat into 'winter quarters', managing, with their usual display of soldierly initiative, to find a partly-furnished house in Pangbourn Drive which its owners were willing to make available rent free, the unit deciding that their occupation made it government property and hence exempt from paying rates. Here the defenders of Canons Park made themselves very comfortable, returning from patrols round the sleeping or blitz-disturbed streets, to a good fire, made from 'the rotten scaffold

19. Home Guard – miners in South Wales.

poles which abounded in the vicinity', their guardroom being easily identifiable in the worst blackout from the pleasant 'smell of chicken broth' emanating from it.

During the hours not on watch, men on overnight duty passed the time in various ways. Cards were a favourite recreation, gossip another. The writer John Lehmann at first 'took a volume or poem or a novel by Conrad' to his headquarters 'in a little converted shop between the local branch of Lloyds Bank and the cinema', but was soon listening instead.

> With innocent amazement to dramatic detail of the more intimate side of village life that had been shrewdly and silently absorbed by the carpenter or builder in the course of their work. Gradually, the quiet, humdrum, respectable facade of the neighbourhood dropped away, and I had glimpses of violent passions... appalling vices... reckless ambitions... and innumerable fantastic evasions of the law....

Although such incidents were rarely mentioned in them, several romantic accounts were written at this time about the satisfaction of standing sentinel over the sleeping countryside. J. B. Priestly broadcast a 'Postscript' in mid-June about his first night's duty 'on top of a high down, with... a parson, a bailiff, a builder, farmers and farm labourers' and the future Poet Laureate, C. Day Lewis, described in even more lyrical vein how he had helped 'to guard the star-lit village'.

The routine of patrols — usually involving two men on duty for two hours, before and after which they slept — soon became monotonous, but was varied by occasional thrills, as on the memorable occasion when 'about midnight word was brought to

20. Home Guard at the Houses of Parliament.

a section commander in Cornwall that a rubber dinghy had been seen in Mawgan Porth Bay' and 'three or four of us hared down the path from the post office to the beach'. Here they were 'surprised and held up', not by the Germans but 'the Trevarrian patrol, who had silently stalked us and taken us in the rear. They had seen the lights of our torches as we had been searching the caves.'

In this thinly populated area most of the excitement, however was provided by nature. A solitary patroller, armed with a shotgun, having 'spied a stranger standing well out in a large field' challenged and finally shot him, only to discover that 'the enemy' was a scarecrow keeping guard over the farmer's potatoes. Other 'parachutists' carefully stalked at this time include sheep, cows and surely the smallest adversary ever to confront a nervous LDV — a stationary hedgehog mistaken in the dim light for the head of a prostrate and cunningly camouflaged soldier.

Partly, no doubt, to keep themselves occupied and awake, many LDVs usurped the job of the air raid wardens, and took to harrowing their fellow citizens over trivial offences against the blackout regulations. In Canons Park, Edgware, enthusiasm for persecuting 'fifth-columnists' showing light rapidly waned after a rifle had been carefully aligned on one particularly blatant beam some distance away and it was found that the offending window belonged to the Platoon headquarters. Real zealots in the hunt for illicit lights deplored what seemed to them the scandalous leniency with which offenders were treated by police and wardens. 'We found one fifth-columnist signalling with a light', complains the same company's history indignantly, 'but the police let him off'. Once the LDV began to acquire arms, however, it was a brave man who argued with them, for many simply shot out (or at least at) bulbs not turned off in response to their shouts.

21. London Home Guard in a public display involving the much cartooned pike.

22. Testing the defences of an airfield, Southern Command.

One LDV commander decided one Sunday late in May 'to impose a curfew to bring home the seriousness of the position to the inhabitants', although the unit's historian admits: 'I don't think the police quite liked this one.' But the LDV were not deterred and — a pleasant historical touch — the 'warning' was duly "cried" through the town by the Town Crier'.

Although most of the citizens of Newquay tamely buckled under to this almost illegal tyranny, one patrol discovered near the sea 'a courting couple on whom the curfew had made no impression. How sternly we held them up at the point of the bayonet, so to speak, and examined their identity cards', one of those concerned remembers. 'We advised them to make all speed for home, but I doubt if they did.' The chronicle of the Wilmington platoon records a typical capture. 'Our leader held them up, demanded their identity cards, and said to the man: "Do you know you have been in a prohibited area?" "Oh no he hasn't", snapped the girl.'

The LDV justified their vigilance on the grounds of the danger from 'fifth columnists', the second great myth produced to explain the collapse of France, and apart from such civilian traitors, it was also believed that enemy troops, or single spies, might be dropped disguised as postmen, railway workers or — most popular of all — nuns. One writer on irregular warfare even passed on his 'hunch that adolescent enemy agents may be dropped in the uniforms of Boy Scouts'. Such fears were complete fantasy. There *were* no fifth columnists. Nor, we now know, did a single German spy land in Britain without being immediately caught. But the country's new guardians were taking no chances. 'It was the LDVs great delight,' wrote one member of a London platoon, 'to pull up all policemen and ask for their identity cards, especially inspectors'. One squad even tried to detain a constable, who refused to comply, while

23. Home Guard on parade, Springfield in Essex.

24. A Home Guard firing through a smoke screen.

he in turn threatened to arrest them for carrying arms without a licence.

If the police found the LDV troublesome, the ordinary motorist soon regarded them as considerably more of a nuisance — at any rate for the moment — than the Germans. The enforced battleground between the two were the roadblocks, which from the end of May onwards became an increasingly familiar feature of the English landscape. 'The earliest roadblocks were pathetic', wrote the colonel who later commanded the 5th (Bideford) Battalion, in Devon, 'consisting of oil drums filled with earth or stones, connected by spars and possibly a scrap of wire. But... they prevailed through the greater part of Period 1' — that is, until the early autumn of 1940. Other obstacles were equally insubstantial. In Kent the earliest were farm carts tipped on end; in West Cornwall 'ploughs and harrows'.

Later defences were more elaborate. Concrete cylinders, usually 3' by 2' in size and weighing 9 cwt were soon a common sight everywhere, and, as many car drivers discovered, came off best in any collision. Other types of road block consisted of smaller concrete pyramids — popularly known as 'Dragon's teeth' — forests of iron or concrete posts, and, probably the most satisfactory of all, 'hairpins', which despite the name needed three or four men to lift them, consisting as they did of bent steel girders, six or eight feet long, which fitted into previously prepared sockets in the roadway. In close support of such positions, commanders sited their fire trenches, from which to bombard the halted enemy transport, but posting men in such positions needed care. 'It is wiser' cautioned one unofficial shilling *Handbook*, 'to have them all on one side of the road in case they all fire on each other at moments of excitement.'

25. In Kent, Major Holdness and his two sons overhaul their equipment.

26. In South Wales Sgt Bill Davies, a miner, sets out to mount guard.

Long before all these formidable obstacles were ready, however, the LDV had taken to challenging drivers with a zest that suggested that many had nursed a life-long ambition to stop the traffic or (sometimes literally) hit back at the much-envied motorist. (At this time fewer than one person in twenty owned a car.) Driving in the blackout was always a strain, especially with signposts removed to confuse enemy parachutists, and being constantly stopped by the LDV was the last straw.

The farmer and broadcaster, A. G. Street, whose platoon in rural Wiltshire took to harassing motorists with enthusiasm, described complacently how pointed remarks about 'grown-up Boy Scouts' and 'playing at soldiers, like a lot of kids' from exasperated motorists did little good:

> After one or two regrettable incidents the public realised that... it was safer to obey... without argument. The man who refused to show his identity card on the grounds that he had shown the damned thing twenty times in the last thirty miles and who swore at those who demanded it, found his car key abstracted, his car pushed to the side of the road, and his person held until the civil police took over and gave him the necessary reprimand. The man who drove on when challenged, thinking that 'these yokels won't dare to shoot' was shot at and usually hit...

Other units were equally complacent about the policy of shooting first and asking questions afterwards, which was to earn for the LDV a unique position as the only army in history to have killed more of its own countrymen than its enemies. The commander of one Buckinghamshire unit, for example, proudly described in its history how 'first blood was drawn by the 4th Battalion', the

27. Some of the duties assigned to Home Guardsmen were not appreciated. From *Home Guard Humour*, 1944.

blood being that of a *British* soldier:

> One evening during the early part of June a car, being at a great speed... failed to stop when the signal was made.... BANG, BANG, went the two rifles. The driver jammed on the brakes and the car skidded to the side of the road, where it stopped.... His field service cap had fallen off and blood was running down his face. The two passengers in the back of the car sat motionless, paralyzed with terror.... A neat round hole in the glass at the back of the car showed where the bullet had entered, passing between the heads of the two on the back seat, removing the cap of the driver and breaking the skin down the whole length of the parting of his hair, finally passing out through the windscreen. The other bullet had evidently gone wide. These... soldiers... anxious to get back to their barracks before the gates were locked... afforded the first rifle practice that the two LDVs had indulged in since the war of 1914-18.

Some motorists however, hit back, like an excise officer whose 'peaked cap and dark uniform' aroused the suspicions of one pair of sentries near Land's End. When stopped, he reached under the dashboard, said 'here is my identity card' and pressed an ugly little automatic into the nearer sentry's stomach. His challengers 'listened, chastened, whilst excisemen explained a better way of holding up a car.'

Inevitably, with nerves stretched tight there were false alarms. the first full-scale alert seems to have been in Cornwall, where on Sunday 26 May one LDV commander was roused at 2.30 a.m. by a message that the invasion had started, and set off to collect all the available rifles: ten elderly Lee-Enfields which had arrived

28. Winston Churchill, who created the Home Guard, wielding a Thompson machine gun.

only the previous day and were now in a cell at Truro Police Station. By 5 a.m. the news had reached Newquay where one platoon commander was awakened by the telephone and a voice hoarse with excitement, yelled.... 'Report to the Drill Hall at once. Enemy parachutes have landed near Dover and planes are moving towards Plymouth.' All this later, and luckily, proved untrue; the 'enemy' observed landing off Kent were parachute mines dropping in the sea.

Having been told to watch for parachutists, the LDV were soon seeing them everywhere. Barrage balloons reflecting the rising sun, searchlights shining on clouds, anti-aircraft bursts, even swans landing in the moonlight, were all reported as paratroops at various times. Occasionally the church bells were rung, the signal that an invasion had begun. In Gloucestershire, where the bells of one village church rang out one evening, and the LDV dashed off on bicycles to their rendezvous, the 'parachutist' turned out to be hay blowing off a stack. Although the police in Stroud angrily telephoned the local warden to 'stop that damned row' the noise continued, for the ringer had locked himself in against the invading Germans and the louder the hammering on the door the more fervently he rang.

The largest and most celebrated false alarm occurred on the night of 7 September, just as the Blitz on London was beginning. The mistake this time was made by the Army, which interpreted the signal *Cromwell*, signifying 'conditions right for invasion', to mean that the assault had actually begun. Over a large stretch of countryside the church bells rang as the panic spread, and every LDV has his own memories of that famous night. These were the experiences of one garage and taxi-service proprietor living in a village near Aylesbury:

29. Local Defence
Volunteers.

I found my mate Busby standing outside the *Black Horse*... We took up our positions at the crossroads...

'Look, here comes our first lot, fire engines.'

'Halt!' we yelled, and bought our guns to the ready. A helmeted fireman leaned from the cab.

'Wot the bleedin' hell are you blokes playin' at?'

'Password!' we demanded.

'London's burning, mates. That's our password. Come on, Bill, let her go, and make 'em jump for it.'

In the next car we stopped, a man in a naval officer's uniform sat at the wheel. We watched him warily as he wound down his driving window... 'Password' and added, a 'please, sir', to be on the safe side. Angrily he reached forward and thrust a leather-bound card into my face.

'Here's my official pass. You're the third lot of Home Guarders who've held me up since I left Aylesbury. Now, do you think I can get along? And for goodness sake stop poking that gun at me — it might go off...'

By now the LDV had a new name, coined by Winston Churchill in a broadcast on the 14 July, when he referred to the existence 'behind the Regular Army' of 'more than a million of the LDV or, as they are much better called, the Home Guard', and this name, an obvious improvement, was formally announced on 23 July 1940. On 3 August, Home Guard units were given 'county' titles, like those of the Regular Army, so that 'the Abingdon Platoon' LDV became 'No. 3 Platoon, "A" Company, 1st Berkshire (Abingdon) Battalion, Home Guard', and it was promised that soon each battalion would receive a shoulder flash and cap badge of its own.

30. & 31. *Top:* LDV volunteers are taught how to throw 'Molotov Cocktails' a practical means of dealing with tanks. *Below:* The effect of one of these 'cocktails' on a dummy tank towed by a car. The bombs, which are bottles partially filled with a mixture of petrol, paraffin and crude oil, were used with much success during the Finnish campaign.

Another sign of the changing times was the introduction of the first badges of rank consisting of from one to four blue stripes on the shoulders for 'officers' and two or three chevrons on the sleeve of 'NCOs', although the use of military rank was still avoided.

The Home Guard's role as part of the Army was set out on 6 August 1940 in Army Council Instruction 924, described by one commanding officer as 'The Magna Carta of the Home Guard'. The changes which now occurred were welcomed by many old soldiers of all ranks, especially the officers, but they came as a blow to recruits attracted by its democratic reputation. The Ministry of Food Home Guard at Colwyn Bay, where orders tended to form the basis for a general discussion, contained both types. 'Some of them', noted one volunteer, 'wanted the unit to be more like His Majesty's Brigade of Guards in the days of King Edward VII; others wanted it to be more like the Red Army in 1917.'

In the end it was the Brigade of Guards which triumphed, and on 6 November 1940 Sir Edward Grigg announced in the House of Commons that the Home Guard 'which has hitherto been largely provisional in character', was to be given 'a firmer and more permanent shape'. It was now, like the Army, to have commissioned officers and NCOs, a fixed organisation, though 'without too much formality of what is called red tape' and — sugaring the pill for the non-military minded — better uniforms and weapons.

And so, nightly awaiting the call to action, the Home Guard settled down to its first winter. The excitement of the summer was over. A long hard slog, with more formality and less fun, lay ahead. If night patrols and guards in mid-summer had often been enjoyable, in November and December they were very different. Henry Smith, Ministry of Food official and Home

Guard Volunteer, wrote this account of what Home Guarding that winter meant in North Wales. His unit had as yet 'no transport... other than overcrowded public vehicles... no commissariat arrangements... rifles, greatcoats, steel helmets and even boots were in short supply.... a kind of primitive communism operated', with the available items being shared out between those on duty. Their job was to guard a quarry hut containing explosives on the seashore near Colwyn Bay:

It blew and rained all that first night. There was no moon and none of the guard, NCOs or privates, had had an opportunity to learn the layout of the quarry. None, therefore, knew the whereabouts of the quarry tramlines, chunks of broken limestone and rain filled potholes, all of which had apparently been set to catch the NCO on his rounds and the sentries on their beat.

On the way home, the conductor of the bus... refusing to accept the statement that the Party were Home Guardsmen coming off duty, stoutly insisted on the rights of the Crosville shareholders. This, however, made no impression on Sgt Balfour who calmly kept his seat saying, 'Yes, indeed you can take it up with whomsoever you like', and proceeded to furnish the irate conductor with the name and address of the unit....

3
After You With The Steel Helmet

One volunteer who lacked a steel helmet, to satisfy a nervous wife left home in the Blitz to come on duty wearing a piece of enamel-wear on his head, secured with a scarf.

North West (London) Frontier. A History of No. 6 Company, 23rd Middlesex Battalion, Home Guard, recalling 1940.

The first sign for one Cornish LDV company that they had not been quite forgotten by the government came at the end of May. One Sunday morning, in the middle of a typical 'flap', 'a tall serious-looking man in a dark grey suit' arrived at the Drill Hall in Newquay and 'having dumped seven Field Service caps (all

6 ⁵/₈) on the table, made off again'. This was the new battalion commander, who having been told that enemy troops were expected at any moment had just received this first instalment of uniform for his men.

The LDV had in fact hardly been formed when it was promised a uniform. '250,000 Field Service caps are available', the minister assured the House of Commons on 22 May, though he said nothing as to sizes, while 90,000 had been distributed and more were to come. What he called 'overalls' the Army called 'denims', an outfit consisting of a coarse, loose-fitting jacket and trousers, worn solely for fatigues. Already, however, in the curious way of the times, one LDV battalion did look like even if they did not yet feel like, soldiers: those in Harrogate, home of the nation's most famous 'popular' tailor, Sir Montague Burton. With financial backing from the local corporation, Sir Montague had turned out, within a week, 1500 sets of well-cut battle-dress, made from officers' quality barathea cloth.

But no other town was as fortunate and while some places received caps but no denims, others received denims, but no caps, and sometimes even the Quartermaster Sergeant himself (although the title was not yet officially in use) could not find a uniform to fit him. *His* first denims, the Company Quarter Master for 'C' Company of the 10th Devonshire Battalion recalls, 'fitted me like a sentry box.... Half the tailors in Torquay were employed juggling with the collars of the blouses and, after cutting about six inches off the bottom of the slacks, things did not look so bad, but we still felt a bit awkward for a while as no Field Service Caps had arrived, and a pork-pie hat did not improve the appearance.'

The chaotic method of distribution defeated even the resourceful members of the 23rd Middlesex Battalion:

32. American Independence Day. A march past of the American Squadron of the Home Guard.

33. After Dunkirk the village barber carried on during periods of guard duty.

Uniforms as they arrived at Platoon were divided by four and sent to the four Sections. It was thus impossible to fit any man. Three pairs of trousers large enough for Göring would arrive with three blouses small enough for Goebbels. It did not matter much, however, as denim never was made to fit human beings. The first parade of the Section after the issue of denim was a sartorial triumph. The necks of the blouses, whatever the size of the blouse itself, were like horse collars and disclosed an array of necks and underwear. One bashful volunteer paraded resplendent in a butterfly collar and black bow tie.

It came as a disagreeable surprise to those who unpacked them to discover that most denims had no fastenings of any kind; the buttons belonging to them arrived separately and were usually of the 'bachelor' type, a form of press stud. Even when fastened up the denims issued were usually far too large. One Plymouth LDV was actually issued with an outsize safety pin to hold up his trousers, which were ten inches too wide around the waist, as well as being eight inches too long in the leg.

The commanding officer of the 4th Buckinghamshire Battalion wrote:

The issue of denim clothing forms a memorable epoch in Home Guard history. If a prize had been offered for the designer of garments that would caricature the human form and present it in its sloppiest and most slovenly aspect, the artist who conceived the Home Guard denim was a class apart. Though marked with different size numbers, it was always a toss-up whether a man resembled an expectant mother or an attenuated scarecrow.

34. Many of the running jokes in the BBC TV series *Dad's Army* were not new. From *Home Guard Humour*, 1944.

'The ridiculous 6 ³/₄ inch sized caps perched on the top of shining craniums' presented another problem. 'One avoided where possible giving the order "about turn" because it was perfectly certain that it would result in the temporary loss of about thirty per cent of the caps' remembers one commander.

Those concerned were only too aware of how they looked as this take-off of *Hamlet* confirms:

August 1940
Enter Armlet in his nightshirt, holding in one hand his newest blue serge suit, and in the other his denim uniform.

To wear or not to wear; that is the question:
Whether 'tis nobler in the mind to suffer
The jeers and titters of misguided females,
Or to slope arms against my natty suitings
And smear my coat with grease; ay, there's the rub
That lends extremity to the long life
My suit was planned for. Yet I should attend
The Office of my denim uniform
I should, in truth, be fearfully arrayed —
(The clumping boots, the empty bosomed tunic,
The calf-revealing armpit-scratching pants,
the neckband sticking out a yard in front,
The trousers sagging out a yard behind) —
The girls would snigger, and the messengers,
looking most reverend and sagely wise
Before me, mock at me behind my back.

Yet if I wear my blue suit on parade
The desperate chance of war might ruin it.
'What dids't thou, daddy, in the Greater War?'
'My son, I got this green stain on my waistcoat
When crawling on my tummy through the grass.'

Fortunately it was not long before the writer ceased 'to itch and sweat beneath the gaberdine', for in the autumn ordinary Army battle-dress began to replace the detested denims. Like other Home Guard equipment it arrived in strange sizes, though where denims had usually been designed for immensely fat men, battle-dress seemed intended for 'men of lamp-post silhouettes'. The local tailors were soon busy carrying out strictly illicit conversions of two 'thin' suits into one normal-sized one. Sometimes blouses and trousers did not match and as the members of A. G. Street's platoon marched uncertainly along the Wiltshire lanes, unkind bystanders would still call out 'Thank God we've got a Navy'. But most men were eager to don their uniform and the arrival of the first sets of battle-dress 'meant headaches and unpopularity for the section leaders', for 'men who turned up regularly' felt they had first claim on the newly-arrived garments, whether they fitted them or not. Even more trouble was caused by ex-officers who insisted on wearing their former uniforms, complete with badges of rank and medal ribbons. 'Nothing in my experience', wrote A. G. Street, 'has infuriated the Home Guards who obeyed orders more than this.... I myself have seen fifty men almost mutinous at the sight of a Home Guard officer flaunting his old uniform.'

The other great source of indignation among early Home Guards was the lack of steel helmets, especially as every air raid warden or ambulance driver possessed one, for a tin hat makes one *feel* safer

CHAPTER I.

Introduction.

1—Objects of the Manual. 2—Role of the Home Guard. 3—Organization. 4—Outline of Training. 5—Drill and Discipline. 6—Co-ordination with the Army. 7—Co-ordination with Other Organizations.

1—Objects of the Manual.

This Manual deals with the organization and training of Home Guard units. It gives unit commanders enough details of elementary training in those branches for which manuals are not readily available to enable them to do effective work. It sets out the details of the new drill when these differ from the drill of twenty years ago, and so will help to get uniformity. A number of minor changes have been made recently by the Army. These have been incorporated, and the drill set out has the approval of the Dominion Commander and so is to be considered the official drill for the Home Guard. It gives working details for the handling of automatic weapons not available for training but possibly available in the field, so that men untrained in the use of these weapons can work them by referring to the manual.

2—Role of the Home Guard.

(A) The primary object of the Home Guard is to have available an organized body of men trained to offer stout resistance in every district, and to meet any military emergency until trained troops can be brought up.

(B) Possible forms of enemy action against this country are, in order of their probability:—
    (i.) Naval action against shipping and land objectives within range of the coast.
    (ii.) Sabotage of the means of production and transport: freezing works, roads and railways, hydro-electric plant, etc.

7

35. Numerous pamphlets and instruction books were published during the war feeding a seemingly insatiable appetite for guidance on how to repel a potential German invasion.

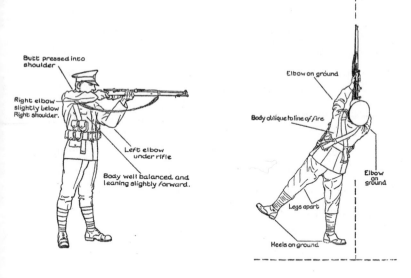

36, 37, 38, & 39. Firing a rifle, from a Home Guard manual.

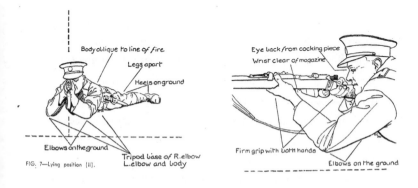

even if it offers little real protection. 'I regret to say', reported the lieutenant-general in charge of organising the Home Guard in the Croydon area, that 'on more than one occasion, I had difficulty in the middle of the night with groups of Home Guards in public shelters, who declined to go out on sentry duty on the grounds that they could not face what were referred to as "showers of shrapnel".' What made the shortage even harder to bear was the steel helmets could be openly bought in the shops. 'The Section Commander', recorded the history of one Middlesex platoon, 'was forced to join a queue of small boys buying them at Gamages, presumably to play soldiers in, and was lucky to secure two', which his men wore in turns when on guard.

In a speech on 6 November 1940, Sir Edward Grigg admitted in the House of Commons that 'there has been a serious shortage of steel helmets for the Home Guard', but promised 'a much larger weekly issue in the near future', and claimed that equipping the Home Guard was otherwise going well. 'Battle-dress', he assured the House, 'will before long be available for the whole Force' and though 'great coats cannot be supplied in adequate numbers before the winter comes on... we have... arranged for a large issue of trench-capes, a warm and serviceable garment made of waterproofed service serge.' A few months later the Home Guard also began to receive other Army-type items of equipment, such as haversacks, ammunition pouches and service-type respirators, which were particularly welcome as a visible sign of superiority to ARP workers, whose gas masks were much less impressive in appearance.

Even when its members at last looked like soldiers, serious Home Guard occasions often continued to be marred by some ludicrous incident. In Bexleyheath an officer reproving one man on his

Bayonet and fore-end clear of cover if possible.

Left hand and forearm rested if cover suitable.

Both elbows rested when possible.

Body pressed against cover.

40. Firing a rifle from behind cover, standing, from a Home Guard manual.

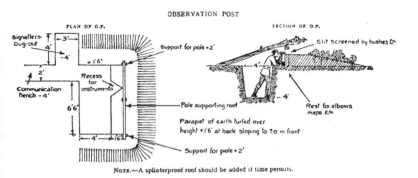

OBSERVATION POST

PLAN OF O.P.

SECTION OF O.P.

Signallers Dug-out

3'

4'

+ 1'6"

Support for pole +2'

Slit screened by bushes Etc

2'

Recess for Instruments

4'

Communication trench - 4'

6'6"

Pole supporting roof

4'

Rest for elbows maps Etc

Parapet of earth turfed over height +1'6' at back sloping to ±o in front

4' 1'6"

Support for pole +2'

NOTE.—A splinterproof roof should be added if time permits.

41. Diagram of an observation post from a Home Guard manual.

doorstep was put firmly in his place by the offender's wife: 'It's three weeks since you cleaned my windows.' In a Gloucestershire town the proud day when the Home Guard acquired their rifles was somewhat marred by the bizarre incident which overtook 'one of the oldest members, whose... long moustaches... unfortunately jammed... in the bolt, and much to his annoyance had to be cut free'. Many were the tales, told too, of the Home Guard's faint-heartedness. In the 2nd Kircudbrightshire Battalion, one man put to judging distance in a field containing some inquisitive heifers, 'made record time to the nearest fence, leaving both rifle and bayonet behind', explaining: 'Sir, I joined the Home Guard to fight Huns, not bloody bulls.' A woman then living in the village of High Brooms in Tunbridge Wells remembers being wakened by 'the terrific yelling outside of a man shouting "Stop! Stop!"' followed by 'the squeal of brakes as a tanker came to a halt. The vocabulary of the driver was unprintable' and not improved when an apologetic voice asked '"Please can you tell me the time?" We found out afterwards it was a young... Home Guard who panicked in the silent gloom and wanted someone to talk to.'

In organisation and titles as well as uniform the Home Guard was, however, by now a military force, barely distinguishable from the Army. The process of change had really begun in November 1940, when in two speeches, on 6th and 19th, the Under-Secretary of State for War announced a drastic reorganisation, with a reduction in routine guard duties, the provision of better weapons and the introduction of military ranks. No one, insisted Sir Edward Grigg, wanted the Home Guard to lose the 'free and easy, homespun, moorland, village-green workshop or pithead character essential to strength and happiness'. But it had grown so fast — to 'something like 1200 battalions, 5000 companies, 25,000 platoons', in fact

SNIPER'S POST.

42. A concealed sniper position
from a Home Guard manual.

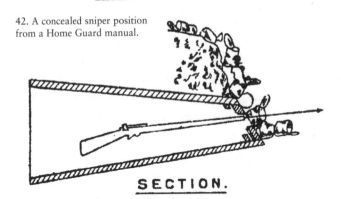

SECTION.

VIEW FROM FRONT.

When front parapet is covered with tins of all kinds, the tin used to disguise the loophole is very difficult to identify even at 10 yds. range

OBLIQUE LOOPHOLE.

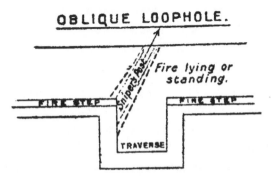

Plenty of Dummy Loopholes should be provided.

about 1,700,000 men, close to its all-time peak — that it needed 'sympathetic attention to its needs and difficulties… to be efficient in its own way, as a volunteer, auxiliary, part-time Force'.

The Home Guard, the minister promised, would now be given a Director General, with a staff of his own at the War Office, responsible to the Commander-in-Chief, Home Forces, Sir Alan Brooke. A full-time officer, receiving an allowance, would be installed to combine the duties of adjutant and quartermaster in each battalion. There would now be proper arrangements 'to cover postage, telephones, clerical assistance and all that sort of thing' to ensure that Home Guards, though unpaid, were not left actually out of pocket.

The second great change announced that November involved the introduction into the Home Guard of military ranks, with the granting of commissions to Home Guard officers, who would be entitled to be saluted and called 'sir'. Unlike his opposite number in the Army, a Home Guard officer would not have 'powers of summary punishment'; a recalcitrant sergeant or delinquent private could only be 'sacked'. The Minister admitted 'there had been criticism' of some of the early appointments of officers and all existing and future officers would now have to go before an independent Selection Board, which would ignore his 'political, business or social affiliations' and consider only his ability 'to command the confidence of all ranks'. One ex-Regular officer found that 'the new system worked very well' and that 'the last two senior approving officers unerringly picked the right potential officer, irrespective of his civilian standing. I saw a gate porter advanced from corporal to platoon commander over the heads of his civilian bosses. I watched a lieutenant rise in eight months to become battalion commander', taking command of men earning

43. Along the cliff edge winds a unit of Home Guard to their posts.

44. Home Guard on patrol in the city.

ten times his salary. 'This scrupulous impartiality on the part of selecting the officers worked a miracle. Discipline reached a level of which many a regular battalion would have been envious, and training leaped ahead.'

Those who failed to be selected or fell victim to the age limit, when commissions began to be listed in February 1941, sometimes stepped down in to the ranks rather than resign. In one unit eighty men handed in their uniforms in protest when their officer was rejected by the Board, while in others the promotion of an unpopular candidate led to resignations. But these un-military gestures, which in the real Army would have been mutiny, were the last demonstration of the old LDV outlook, for in November 1941 the government announced that conscription would be used to keep the Home Guard up to strength, even though at 1,530,000, it was still three times as large as originally intended and Hitler was now deeply embroiled in Russia. Under the National Service (No. 2) Act, any male civilian aged from eighteen to fifty-one could, from January 1942, be ordered to join the Home Guard and to attend for up to forty-eight hours training or guard duties a month, under penalty of a month in jail, or a £10 fine. Once 'in', he could not leave until he was sixty-five though existing volunteers were given until 16 February 1942 to make up their minds whether to stay under the new conditions, or to resign with, if they were under fifty-one, the possibility of being 'directed' back in again.

Some did resign, though not as many as the Government had feared, and usually because they were unable, or unwilling, to tie themselves down to regular attendance in future. During 1941 180,000 men had already left the Home Guard, of whom 60 per cent had joined the Forces, 20 per cent had been expelled, usually for non-attendance, and 20 per cent had resigned, sometime due to

45. Home Guard unit on a tactical
exercise on one of England's beaches in
preparation for any attack.

age. In February 1942 there was no sudden exodus, but gradually thereafter the Home Guard became more and more an army of conscripts. Direction, which had been intended to apply only to certain areas particularly short of men, was soon in force almost everywhere.

Many 'directed men', as they were called, made the best of things; being sentenced to serve in the Home Guard was better, after all, than having to join the Army. Some applied for exemption to an Appeals Board and these became notorious for their leniency. The government was, understandably, not anxious to advertise how many men actually 'dodged the column' and statistics are hard to come by, but it seems doubtful if more than half of the 946,000 'directions' issued between January 1942 and September 1944 were enforced.

As the Home Guard became better organised and the supply of weapons and equipment increased the flow of paper inevitably rose with it, as one member of a Berkshire battalion described:

Daily there descended upon us a shower of letters, forms, chits, returns and memos from battalion HQ. There were the usual military orders.... There was the same old iron ration... missing for eighteen months and doomed so to be for all eternity; the odd gaiter that was surplus to stores and which nobody would own; the slab of chocolate short in a box of a hundred of its kind and which, after many moons, the company QMS in a flash of genius, wrote off with the unassailable alibi, 'destroyed by mice'.

As the Germans never reached Esher the most notable battle recorded in the war diary of the 'Hawker' Platoon of the 53rd Surrey battalion was that of Private Barnacle's Boots. Barney, as his

46. Armed Home Guard patrolling a railway line.

workmates knew him, had already been guilty of such unmilitary acts as throwing a grenade without removing the pin and going to sleep on duty. Now he had committed a far more unpardonable offence: upsetting the official records of clothing issued.

The unfortunate Barnacle had got his boots wet during an exercise and, on reaching home, left them on the stove to dry. Many hours later, when he returned to remove them, all that was left was a charred mass of smouldering leather. The Platoon Quartermaster was informed and the sad story had to be related to the Company Quartermaster. He in turn communicated with the Battalion Quartermaster, whose duty it became to describe the affair to the Surrey Territorial Association. The next stage was a request for the 'remains', as the last visible form of Pte Barnacle's boots was termed. These were not forthcoming, since Pte Barnacle had felt that their days of usefulness had passed and had destroyed them. An impassioned correspondence might easily have developed at this point, but Pte Barnacle was allowed to bring the matter to a close by making a small cash payment which covered the cost of the boots with deductions for legitimate depreciation.

4
Mind My Pike!

A Home Guard weapon was one that was dangerous to the enemy and, to a greater degree, to the operator.

LIEUT-COLONEL J. LEE, *Early Days in the Home Guard,* recalling 1940

Of all the images of the early days of the Home Guard which remain in my memory one stands out: the sight of an older boy at my school, who had just joined it, lovingly whittling down a large piece of wood into a club, with string wound tightly round it to form a handle, and as the final touch, a set of heavy football-boot studs screwed into the 'business' end. Any German he encountered at close quarters was not merely likely to retire hurt, but looking as though he had been badly trodden on in a particularly vicious rugger scrum.

The legend of untrained civilians setting out to confront the invader with golf clubs, carving knives and pitchforks is now as much a part of British history as King Alfred and the cakes, more so in fact since it unquestionably happened. A Banstead woman still remembers her father going on parade flourishing a chair leg and a Worcester Park woman treasures the 'dummy wooden gun' with which her husband stood guard at Guildford. The range of 'blunt instruments', to use the police term, acquired by various individual LDVs and Home Guards was extraordinary. At the very beginning one could sometimes tell a man's trade by the weapon he carried: there were miners in Lancashire patrolling with crowbars, textile-workers with sharpened mill-spindles (some were even made by one enterprising engineer into Swordsticks for the 'officers') labourers with pick-axes, farm workers with pitchforks. A Manchester engineering company added to its usual list of products 'a six-foot spear and a heavily-weighted truncheon' for use by employees. Those of another London factory turned out a supply of 'devastatingly formidable coshes and first-class sticking knives... from rejected scrap materials.... The boss knew all about it. They asked him if they could stay on and use the various tools required after work.... He consented on condition that they gave him the first cosh made.' Clerks and office-workers were at a disadvantage, but not wholly defenceless. The General Post Office, issued a directive in June 1940 advising that, pending the arrival of anything better, guards on its premises should arm themselves with hammers and crowbars, which, it was suggested, 'could usefully be supplemented by a packet of pepper, to interfere with the vision of any persistent unwelcome visitor who tries to force an entry', though this was only recommended as 'a preliminary to other action of a more lasting character'.

47. Home Guards prepare to deal with an 'invader' by means of Molotov coc

48. Regular instructors instruct Home Guardsmen in the use of the 'sticky' bo other up-to-date anti-tank devices.

But everyone wanted something that looked like a firearm, even if it would not actually fire. An Essex unit possessed some fowling pieces and blunderbusses. Fifty ancient Lee-Enfield rifles were 'borrowed' from the *Drury Lane Theatre*, where they had often featured in patriotic tableaux, to give the performance of their life, with the Marylebone Home Guard. The 11th Shropshire Battalion were grateful for some rusty Crimean War cavalry carbines. The 49th Lancashire Battalion raided the BelleVue Zoo in Manchester for old Snyder rifles, which had last seen service nearly a century before. Galleries all over the country, from the Imperial War Museum in London to small local establishments, were combed for ancient arms which could at least be used for training these recruits who did not yet know what a machine gun or hand grenade looked like.

Before long the average LDV unit could probably have mounted from its own resources an impressive history of firearms through the ages. The future 9th Somerset (Wells) Battalion had patrols scouring the Mendip Hills as early as 15 May carrying shotguns, sporting rifles and even elephant guns. In Buckinghamshire, any Germans who advanced via the Aylesbury area were also in for a hot reception. 'Our orders were to arm ourselves with cudgels or heavy walking sticks,' remembers one early volunteer, but 'one "sportsman" carried a boar-spear with a long bamboo shaft with which he was wont to hopefully prod the bramble patches and potentially concealing undergrowth.'

Many of the weapons carried resulted from a public appeal which yielded 20,000 of varying vintages. 'Those handed in' near Marlow, remembers one future officer, 'ranged from pairs of guns in their brass-bound leather cases, the product of makers

49. A 'sticky bomb'.

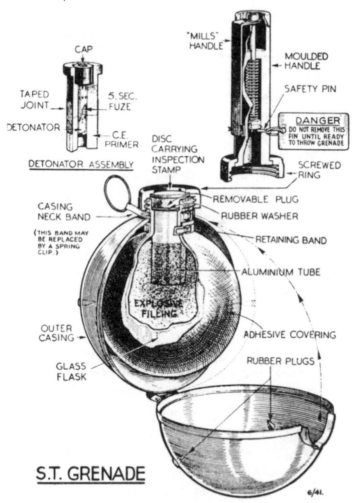

CAP

TAPED JOINT

DETONATOR

5. SEC. FUZE

C.E. PRIMER

DETONATOR ASSEMBLY

"MILLS" HANDLE

MOULDED HANDLE

SAFETY PIN

DANGER
DO NOT REMOVE THIS
PIN UNTIL READY
TO THROW GRENADE

DISC CARRYING INSPECTION STAMP

SCREWED RING

REMOVABLE PLUG

RUBBER WASHER

CASING NECK BAND

(THIS BAND MAY
BE REPLACED
BY A SPRING
CLIP.)

RETAINING BAND

ALUMINIUM TUBE

EXPLOSIVE FILLING

OUTER CASING

ADHESIVE COVERING

RUBBER PLUGS

GLASS FLASK

S.T. GRENADE

6/41.

whose names are household words in the shooting world, down to nondescript weapons of no recorded ancestry....' The shortage here, as in so many places, was made good by private generosity, for 'one of the very first steps taken by the colonel had been to secure a priority delivery from his gun maker of a large supply of man-killing 12-bore cartridges'. Though no German ever set foot in Buckinghamshire, except as a prisoner, 'when ammunition was withdrawn after "Stand-down" only one in ten of these were forthcoming, and many a rabbit had paid the penalty of crossing the path of a dusk-to-dawn patrol'.

This was certainly not the only area where the Home Guard achieved some unofficial target practice of this kind. The wife of a Home Guard lieutenant in the Somerset village of East Coker, recalls how the meat ration 'was helped out by the rabbits caught by the Home Guard on duty', while another battalion's 'wood-combing exercise', at Christmas 1941, flushed out no parachutists but did yield one edible deer as well as a dead fox.

At first, however dangerous to small animals, shotgun armed patrols were not much of a threat to the Germans, for their ammunition, consisting of small pellets, would, according to one authority, 'seldom stop a man at twenty yards'. The government issued some ball cartridges supposed to fit shotguns, but despite the 'strict orders... that the barrels of any shotgun must be tested' before using it, 'it was very difficult indeed' one commander found, to get this done, since 'using the wrong ammunition was a sure way to spoil a good gun'. One platoon near Aylesbury did, however, carry out its own trials, and having removed the pellets from a 'conventional cartridge substituted a single lead ball. As proof of its efficiency, we blew the village cricket club scoreboard into matchwood with two or three trial rounds'. Other shotgun

50. The comic possibilities of the 'sticky bomb' from *Home Guard Humour*, 1944.

owners hastened to follow suit and 'many a... barrel was ruined in consequence.'

The first issue of military rifles began within a few days in the danger areas: in Kent, for example, there were already 1500 armed men on guard by 21.00 hours on Saturday 18 May, and before long most of those near the coast had received some rifles, though a 'full issue' tended to be one to every two men. Units further inland received even fewer. The standard 'ration' for government departments was ten rifles; at the Ministry of Food headquarters these had to serve 500 volunteers. At Sidcup the first dozen rifles received were distributed democratically by ballot. One member of a six-man patrol in another London Suburb remembers being selected to carry their own rifle as he had been a cadet in the First World War.

Automatic and long-range weapons were at this time almost totally lacking, but Home Guard inventors did their best to fill the gap. The 'Hawker' platoon of the 53rd Surrey's, near Esher, prepared blueprints for a grenade catapult, operated by a man lying on his back with a length of strong elastic stretched between his feet. It was, alas never built; but another unit, in Sussex, not merely made but proudly demonstrated to the Under Secretary of State for War a wooden crossbow designed to fire a grenade fifty yards. To the same near-fantasy world belongs the 'flamethrower' produced at Houghton-le-Spring in Durham, which sprayed an advancing enemy with inflammable dry-cleaning fluid through a stirrup-pump.

The problem of hitting enemy armour troubled many Home Guards. One despairing suggestion was for metal soup plates to be placed face-down in the road, so that the crew would assume them to be mines and stop to remove them. But the anti-tank

51. & 52. Grenade throwing needs practice, (top) whether as here with the 36M grenade or (below) with Molotov cocktails.

weapon which became almost the Home Guard's trademark was the Molotov cocktail — a name coined in Finland a few months earlier, where men would remark 'That's one for Molotov', the Russian Foreign Minister, as they hurled each missile. The Molotov basically consisted of about a pint of inflammable liquid in a bottle, with a piece of flannel soaked in paraffin protruding from the neck as a fuse. Its range was only from 5 to 15 yards, and although it was an unreliable, as well as a dangerous weapon, Molotov-manufacture was soon in full swing. It perhaps appealed to those who in peacetime produced homemade wine; one man in Buckinghamshire eventually had 1000 in his garden.

Their chief value was, however, psychological, for the person most likely to suffer from a Molotov was the user, like an officer in Cambridgeshire:

On one occasion a platoon commander had just thrown one of these missiles and was explaining to his men that they were foolproof... [when] Private Buggins stepped forward from the ranks, halted three paces from the platoon commander and saluted smartly. 'Yes Buggins?' 'Excuse me, sir, your breeches are on fire!'

The first real weapons to reach the LDV in any quantity were half a million ancient rifles, sent by the United States during June and July in response to an appeal from Winston Churchill. Their vintage was betrayed by their popular name 'Springfield 1917', or '17' for short, and they arrived caked in the heavy grease, like congealed vaseline, which had protected them during their long years of disuse. Removing the grease proved to be a dirty and wearisome job.

Opinions about the Springfields varied. One experienced

53. A farmer from Oxfordshire getting ready for a parade.

ex-officer considered, 'we might have been much worse served', though the weapon was 'rather cumbersome' with 'a difficult bolt action for rapid fire'. But the rifle's real disadvantage was that it fired .300 ammunition instead of the standard .303, and to prevent the wrong calibre being used a red band was painted around the barrel. Another foreign rifle distributed at this time, the Canadian Ross, was of standard calibre, but, as one user noted, 'unsuitable for Service conditions as… any earth or dirt may cause a jam.' Another veteran, whose platoon in Devon possessed ten Ross rifles between sixty men, regarded it as 'a grand shooting rifle, but… a heavy, ill-balanced brute to lug about'. He was delighted when their Ross's were replaced by 'light, handy and accurate' Remingtons. Unfortunately, however, with only fifty rounds per weapon, 'we had enough ammunition, for, at a liberal estimate, half an hour's battle' so none could be spared for firing on the range.

The Home Guard did however manage to get some unofficial practice, mainly at motorists who were frequently killed or injured because the inexperienced user, aiming at a wheel, had made no allowance for the weapon jerking upwards as he fired. Considering the casual way in which many Home Guards treated firearms it is remarkable there were not more accidents.

Every unit soon had its tale of narrow escapes, like the 3rd Cambridgeshire and Ely Battalion, where 'an agitated volunteer reported that he had put a round through somebody's electric stove'. Although it had 'wrecked the inside of the oven and made its exit through the back, the owner behaved like a brick, made no claim and let the matter drop'. Not long afterwards another man fired his rifle by mistake, and 'the bullet went through a man's bedroom and out by the roof. The man was in bed with his wife

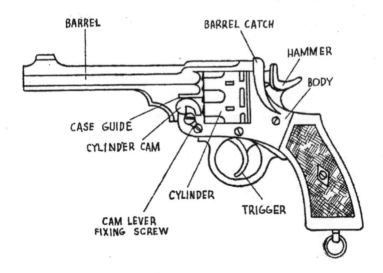

54. & 55. (top) Webley pistol .45 inch or .38 inch and (below) diagram showing the parts of government issue rifle from a Home Guard manual.

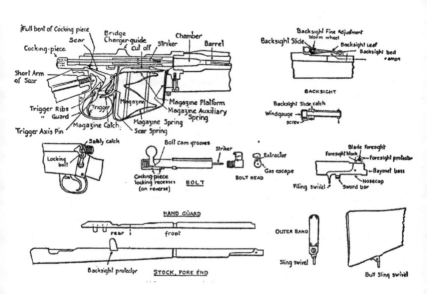

and was actually heard to say "Get up, missus, the ------- are here at last:".' Lance Corporal Ernest Raymond watched horrified when one 'rusty and paunched veteran', advancing to a homemade range in a sand pit on Hampstead Heath 'in a moment of abstraction and apprehension... drew on the trigger while... still walking' so that 'a bullet shot high into the sky... over the trees of Ken Wood'.

The weapon for which every old soldier longed was the standard rifle which had served the British Arms so well in the First World War and was, in an updated version, to become its 'workhorse' in the Second — the .303 Short Magazine Lee-Enfield (SMLE), or its slightly heavier and longer, but more accurate cousin, the P14. The SMLE, at 8 Ib 6 oz, weighed a pound less than the Ross, was accurate up to 1600 yards, and was exceedingly reliable and easy to operate in the hands of a trained man.

By the end of 1940 many units had at least a few Lee-Enfields, though it was to be another year or more before they were plentiful everywhere. By this time some automatic weapons had also begun to arrive. The first received by one West Country unit was a Lewis gun, mounted on a pivot and tripod behind which its two-man crew squatted, swinging it freely across their front, as it poured out 600 bullets a minute. For heavier support this battalion relied on a Hotchkiss of very ancient vintage, and a veteran swore that he recognised it as an old friend of the South African campaign.

Far more popular was the BAR, Browning Automatic Rifle (or light machine gun), with which a skilled man could fire 40 single shots a minute, though on 'automatic' its rate of fire was up to 550 rounds. At under 16 Ib in weight this was a one-man weapon, but there was a heavier two-man version providing double the rate of fire, and during 1941 this largely replaced the popular but far

56. & 57. Home Guards are instructed in the use of the Lewis machine gun (top). The Lewis light machine gun from a Home Guard manual (below).

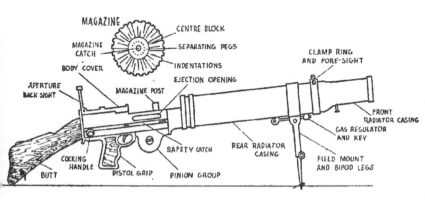

more bulky Vickers, which with its cooling jacket weighed 43 Ib. The Browning , one officer found, 'fired well when properly water-cooled' but 'when overheated gave us some exciting moments'. 'My own opinion', declared the colonel of a West Cornwall battalion, 'is that the Vickers would stand up to the bowling better.'

When a new weapon arrived the keenest Home Guards could barely wait to get their hands on it. One garage mechanic from near Aylesbury recalls 'being summoned to the platoon commander's house to assist in the reassembling of a Browning automatic', only to be confronted on arrival with 'a scatter of spare parts strewn on the lounge carpet' and 'the skeleton of the sub-machine gun... in an armchair'. Its owner, had managed to strip the gun so effectively that he was now unable to reassemble it.

A weapon whose appearance was familiar to every filmgoer was the Thompson sub-machine-gun, a formidable and easily carried weapon that fired 600 heavy calibre rounds a minute. So much prestige gathered round this sinister device that one writer pointed out reassuringly that 'no tommy-gun can possibly hit you at 500 yards', though he rather spoilt this by adding: 'at 100 yards or less it will cut you to pieces within two seconds.' According to this writer the British Army lacked tommy-guns because, as one general put it: 'We do not intend to introduce the methods of the Chicago gangster into European warfare.' In 1941 tommy-guns were no sooner issued than they were withdrawn again for use by the Commandos; but soon afterwards the Home Guard received a new automatic weapon, the Sten, widely used by the resistance movements in Europe. It consisted of a crude combination of wooden stock (later replaced by 'T' shaped metal) and unfinished-looking black steel. One expert described it as a 'spout, a handle

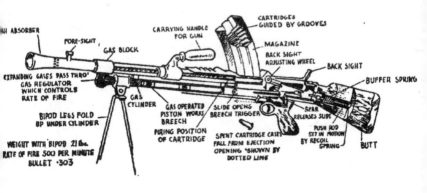

Labels (top diagram – Bren light machine gun):
SHOCK ABSORBER · FORE-SIGHT · GAS BLOCK · CARRYING HANDLE FOR GUN · CARTRIDGES GUIDED BY GROOVES · MAGAZINE · BACK SIGHT ADJUSTING WHEEL · BACK SIGHT · BUFFER SPRING · EXPANDING GASES PASS THRO' GAS REGULATOR WHICH CONTROLS RATE OF FIRE · GAS CYLINDER · GAS OPERATED PISTON WORKS BREECH · SLIDE OPENS BREECH TRIGGER · SEAR RELEASES SLIDE · PUSH ROD SET IN MOTION BY RECOIL SPRING · BUTT · BIPOD LEGS FOLD UP UNDER CYLINDER · FIRING POSITION OF CARTRIDGE · SPENT CARTRIDGE CASE FALL FROM EJECTION OPENING "SHOWN BY DOTTED LINE" · WEIGHT WITH BIPOD 21 lbs. RATE OF FIRE 500 PER MINUTE BULLET ·303

58. & 59. (top) The Bren light machine gun, (below) the Thompson sub-machine gun .45 inch from a Home Guard manual.

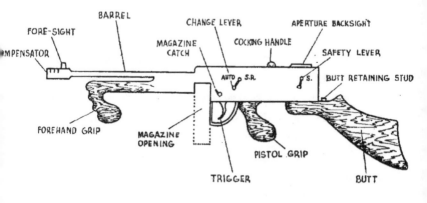

Labels (bottom diagram – Thompson sub-machine gun):
FORE-SIGHT · BARREL · CHANGE LEVER · APERTURE BACKSIGHT · COMPENSATOR · MAGAZINE CATCH · COCKING HANDLE · SAFETY LEVER · AUTO · S.R. · S. · BUTT RETAINING STUD · FOREHAND GRIP · MAGAZINE OPENING · TRIGGER · PISTOL GRIP · BUTT

and a tin box'. 'The day our platoon was issued with Sten guns', remembers one Edinburgh Home Guard, 'I knew we were going to win the war. "At Last", I thought, "we've ditched the fine British craftsmanship nonsense".' Most users of the Sten, however, soon decided that there was something to be said for fine British craftsmanship. 'They were said to cost 30s each and I do not doubt it', commented one Cornish officer. 'It is inaccurate over 50 yards and apt to be dangerous in the hands of an untrained man.' 'It's breeding might be described as by Woolworth out of Scrap Heap', agreed another Home Guard in Devon. 'It works... I am told, after being thrown into a river and dragged through mud.'

Undoubtedly the most famous, and despised, of all Home Guard weapons was the pike, issued in the autumn of 1941, by which time most units were well armed. Although humourists took to calling out 'Gadzooks!' as pike-bearing Home Guards appeared in public (which they did not do for long) the pikes bore little resemblance to their ancient forebears. The Home Guard version was more a gas pipe than a true pike, consisting of a 3'6" length of 2" metal piping, weighing 5 lb, with a 17" bayonet fitted into the end. When they first arrived many commanders tried to keep even their existence dark. 'The egregious pike never went beyond the battalion HQ store', recalls one Buckinghamshire colonel.

The official explanation for issuing pikes was they would be useful for street fighting, and one unit was photographed skilfully parrying blows while storming houses. The picture appeared in the press over the caption 'Mind my Pike!', recalling the current catchphrase of the comedian Jack Warner, 'Mind my bike!'

In the House of Lords, in March 1942, one Home Guard peer complained of the waste of '1000 tons of valuable iron and steel' on a weapon which its intended users regarded 'as little more than

Plate 1. Official War Artist Eric Kennington travelled the length and breadth of Britain during 1942-3 to capture the essence of spirit of the Home Guard. Here is his portrait of Corporal Robertson, City of Edinburgh Home Guard. Portrait by Eric Kennington.

Plate 2. Anti-aircraft gunners, London Home Guard.
Eric Kennington.

Plate 3. Sergeant Bluett, Cornwall Home Guard. Portrait by Eric Kennington.

Plate 4. LDV River Severn Patrol.

Opposite: Plate 5. Firing a rifle from behind cover, kneeling and lying, from a Home Guard manual.

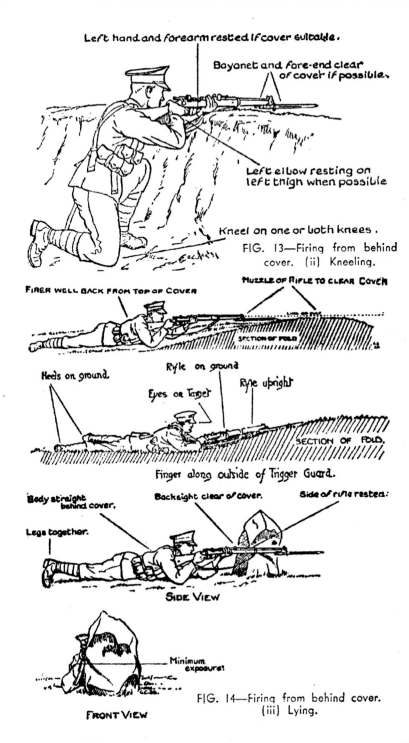

Left hand and forearm rested if cover suitable.

Bayonet and fore-end clear of cover if possible.

Left elbow resting on left thigh when possible

Kneel on one or both knees.

FIG. 13—Firing from behind cover. (ii) Kneeling.

FIRER WELL BACK FROM TOP OF COVER

MUZZLE OF RIFLE TO CLEAR COVER

SECTION OF FOLD

Heels on ground.

Rifle on ground

Rifle upright

Eyes on Target

SECTION OF FOLD.

Finger along outside of Trigger Guard.

Body straight behind cover.

Backsight clear of cover.

Side of rifle rested.

Legs together.

SIDE VIEW

Minimum exposure.

FRONT VIEW

FIG. 14—Firing from behind cover. (iii) Lying.

HOME GUARD

GUARD

Humour

1/6

DURING FOUR AND A HALF YEARS

With the
HOME GUARD

2/6

By

CAPTAIN SIMON FINE

The

HOME GUARD

POCKET MANUAL

Price 6d.
No. 392
Tenth Edition.

Previous page spread left: Plate 6. The Home Guard was truly a mass organization and spawned a mini publishing industry, this is the cover of a 1944 'toilet' book, *Home Guard Humour.*

Previous page spread right: Plate 7. The cover of the 1944 memoir, *With the Home Guard* by Home Guardsman Captain Simon Fine.

Plate 8. Cover of one of the many Home Guard manuals produced during the war.

Opposite: Plate 9. Battery Sergeant-Major Dawson, Yorkshire Home Guard. Portrait by Eric Kennington.

Above: Plate 10. Home Guard training.

Plate 11. An instructor demonstrates how to use the 'cup discharger'. A platoon commander uses one.

Plate 12. A Home Guard sniper in camouflage.

Plate 14. Sergeant Hampshire, Middlesex Home Guard. Portrait by Eric Kennington.

Opposite: Plate 13. Coast Defense Gunners, Lancashire Home Guard. Eric Kennington.

Image on next page spread left: Plate 15. Company Sergeant-Major Waters, Lancashire Home Guard. Portrait by Eric Kennington.

Image on next page spread right: Plate 16. Coast Defence searchlight, Lancashire Home Guard. Eric Kennington.

Plate 17. 'They don't like it up "em"'. Home Guard Corporal Charles Batchelor could have said.

60. Home Guardsmen learning how to use new automatic machine guns.

61. An instructor demonstrates how to use the 'cup discharger' for grenades.

an insult' and in the end the sole person ever harmed by a pike was the minister responsible, whose reputation never recovered. Only one unit ever seems to have employed them, a platoon at Canons Park who faced the task of clearing up 'after the Home Guard gala with side-shows in 1941' when '2000 people left an enormous mount of litter.... We cleared the ground in half an hour by the simple process of arming each man with a pike and a sandbag. As each man went forward he impaled all pieces of paper on his pike and transferred them to his sandbag'.

For fighting at close quarters the Home Guard by now possessed bayonets — though usually the old-fashioned 'carving knife' type rather than the shorter 'meat skewer' now being issued to the Army — and an ample supply of grenades, particularly the No. 36 HE, known to old soldiers as the Mills bomb. As it was lethal up to twenty yards, farther than many an unpracticed arm could throw it, grenade-throwing could be a trying experience to all concerned, as one Ministry of Food Home Guard discovered:

I executed the perfect overarm with all my strength behind it. Something went wrong. My hand and the Mills refused to part company at the right moment. But... full of wishful thinking, I looked over the parapet at the target hole, expecting to see the grenade lying on the bulls-eye. It wasn't there.... No sign anywhere. And then, three feet away, half left, I spotted... this object stuck in the mud. Somehow it didn't make sense that this was a grenade, let alone my grenade... Just as I did awaken to stark reality a whistle rang out.... Officer, sergeant and private got down behind Mother Earth, all very close to the ground. The next second our eardrums were almost split by the explosion and we three were subjected to premature burial. The officer and sergeant... thanked me for the

62. Home Guard armoured cars on patrol in the North of Scotland.

63. This Rolls Royce monster, donated to the Home Guard, was converted by the men themselves.

unusual experience, but the very red-faced NCO in the priming pit offered to pay my fare to Broadmoor.

By the end of 1941, although homemade devices were now forbidden, and even the faithful Molotov cocktail had been 'stood down' unless used with an 'official' self-igniting bomb, the Home Guard had an impressive armoury of fourteen different varieties of bombs and grenades. They could be used for starting fires, making smoke screens, signalling by day or by night and, most important of all, hurling at tanks and enemy infantry. Although the Army referred to these devices by numbers and initials, to the Home Guard they were the 'thermos bomb', so called because of its shape, 'the talcum power grenade', originally made from requisitioned cosmetic cans, and the 'sticky bomb' designed, when the cover was removed, to cling to a tank and penetrate armour an inch thick. Almost all these missiles had one — possibly fatal — weakness, they had to be thrown, often by an inexperienced or elderly arm. To overcome this problem the Army produced several ingenious — if even more dangerous — devices, such as the 'EY rifle projector', named after Edward Yule, its inventor. The device consisted of a 'cup discharger' fitted on the end of an ordinary rifle equipped with special cartridge, which fired various types of grenade, including anti-tank missiles, from 80 to 200 yards.

An altogether larger and grander version of the same basic idea was the Northover projector, which resembled a large drainpipe mounted on twin legs. The Northover was the pride of my school company, though firing it was a 'treat reserved for the masters' platoon'. Henry Smith had mixed feelings about it:

The principal purpose for which it was designed was to discharge

64. Cumberland Home Guard tensed for the word 'fire' behind a Spigot Mortar, one of the Home Guards' formidable pieces of sub-artillery.

65. On the anniversary of the birth of the Home Guard, demonstration teams fire the Northover projector in the heart of London.

glass bottles containing a phosphorous mixture which burst into livid flames, giving off quantities of suffocating smoke upon exposure to the air. When dealing with this ammunition... the least lovable characteristics of the Northover projector became apparent. Unless the utmost care was exercised in loading and firing there was a natural tendency for the shock of discharge to break the glass bottles in the breech, whereupon the gun, and sometimes the gunner and troops standing to leeward, were liable to burst into flames.

In 1943, battalions received the medieval-sounding Blacker-Bombard, later given the more prosaic name of the Spigot Mortar, an ugly-looking short-barrelled weapon, which could fire a 14 Ib bomb nearly 800 yards and a 20 Ib one 450, though it was most effective between 75 and 100 yards. The Spigot Mortar was, claimed one enthusiastic officer, 'quite an artillery piece, firing either anti-tank or anti-personnel bombs with remarkable accuracy'. Unfortunately neither the Northover nor the Spigot was truly mobile, though, in the best Home Guard tradition, many units produced homemade trolleys for both weapons, rather like those used by golfers.

At last, in 1943 the Home Guard received a weapon that did bear some resemblance to a 'real' field gun and could be towed into action behind even a 7 h.p. 'baby' Austin. The Smith Gun could hurl a 10 Ib projectile over 1000 yards and its appearance was enough to put any enemy gunner off his stroke, for it 'had to be turned upside down [almost] before it could be fired'. The crew's first action was, in fact, to tip the weapon on its side, whereupon the lower wheel provided the firing platform, and the upper one a bulletproof shield.

66. Brigadier General J.V. Campbell, VC, who commanded a Gloucestershire battalion, inspects the new issue of sten guns.

12. TYPICAL TANK AMBUSH.

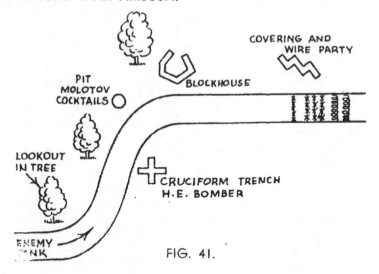

FIG. 41.

67. Diagram showing a typical tank ambush from a Home Guard manual.

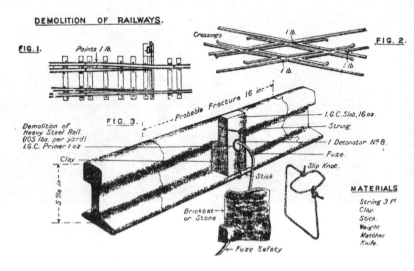

68. Use of explosive to sabotage railways from a Home Guard manual.

In 1940 the principal weapon against enemy tanks would have been burning oil and petrol. The steep and narrow lanes of the West Country, hemmed in by tall hedges, were ideal for such defences. Typical was Bideford in Devon where:

> Two petrol tanks fed pipes whence a spray of petrol could be directed on to vehicles halted or hesitating just in front of the blocks; these were known as 'flame traps'. One of these… was tested to the huge delight of a crowd of local residents which rapidly assembled when the presence of the NFS [National Fire Service] indicated the likelihood of an exciting event. The flame trap worked perfectly.

For mobile use there was soon the Harvey Flame Thrower, a hand-pump operated device which was a direct, if more 'legitimate', descendant of the stirrup-pump flame-throwers of earlier days. This was supplemented by the graphically-named Hedgehopper, an oil-drum with a built in charge designed to hurl it over a wall, though it could all too easily cause consternation, if nothing worse, by immediately bouncing back on the defenders. The Home Guard's basic flame weapon, which survived throughout the war, was the oddly named Fougasse, an oil drum built into the roadside, which sprayed out a jet of flame when fired, at first by pulling a piece of string. Later versions were more sophisticated and Bideford, for example, had ten 'which could be fired by electric circuits under remote control'. Like so many Home Guard weapons the famous Fougasse was never fired in anger, but it is commemorated by surely the worst pun of the entire war — the unit magazine of the 2nd Lanarkshire battalion was excruciatingly named: *Phew, Gas!*

5
Waiting For Jerry

Every day that passes brings nearer the time when the enemy will attempt invasion and when that time comes... we must be prepared to give a good account of ourselves.... We must all strive to qualify ourselves to give Jerry a perfectly appalling time should he have the temerity to land in this country.

LIEUT-COLONEL D. C. CROMBIE, *Order of the Day* to the 5th (Bideford) Battalion, Devon Home Guard, 31 December 1941.

'Like playing Indians but with a real rifle.' This comment by one very young Home Guard, in a factory unit in Surrey, sums up the attitude of some un-military minded recruits. About most training in the early days there was, despite the nation's dangers, an air of enjoyment. The humourists who accused the Home Guard of 'playing at soldiers' were not wholly wide of the mark — and in the summer of 1940 there was no more suitable game to play.

In offices the first training session often took place after work in a conference room, or on any stretch of flat roof — the most easily-available open space — for shortage of training areas provided to be a constant problem for units in cities. The Ministry of Food LDV, when formed in Westminster, found themselves, as 'non-members', charged a shilling a head for use of the range belonging to the Ministry Rifle Club. 'Units operating in big cities', admits one NCO in Marylebone, 'held parades at times carefully chosen to avoid the vigilance of Park Superintendents.' A Liverpool woman remembers her father returning, disgusted, from one early parade. His unit's attempts to train on a patch of waste ground had been defeated by small boys enjoying cricket who had driven them off with the reproachful cry: 'But, mister, we was playing 'ere first.'

There were the experiences of one middle-aged volunteer in Haywards Heath, where 300 men had come forward:

> We split into sections and were drilled by an ancient 'dug-out' NCO in a yard behind the YMCA hut. Motley sections we were, most of us over fifty and some of us far too fat. In the absence of... rifles we were given flat wooden slabs, cut more or less into a rifle's shape; and with these our old NCO (in a trilby hat) taught us how to slope arms, ground arms, port and even present arms to him, as he walked past us with the port and the hauteur (as he conceived them) of a Commander-in-chief. In the long summer evenings — and what a summer that was in 1940, radiant and calm and ever un-fading over the fields of England — we gambolled about the countryside in extended order and sometimes flung ourselves on our bellies (though 'flung' is too flattering a word for many of us)

69. Home Guard in training.

so as to practise firing at a deep and wide tank-trap dug across our meadows.... So did Britain begin her warfare against the most magnificently organised army on earth.

It was not until November 1940, with the danger of immediate invasion clearly over, that systematic training on a national scale began for the Home Guard. 'With the longer nights', explained the Under-Secretary for War in the House of Commons on 6 November, 'when normal employment overruns both dawn and dusk, it cannot maintain its summer standard of vigilance.... Watches, in-lying pickets and patrols can be limited to such as can be maintained on a shift system by those who can afford the time. Needless picketing or patrolling should be discouraged, and attention turned to training instead.' Two weeks later, he announced that a full-time Army instructor would be attached to each battalion, but that the Home Guard would have to provide most of its own teachers. It was, he declared, 'simply full of talent' and this rapidly proved true, as one recently retired 'Regular' now attached to the Home Guard in London discovered, when he assembled his instructors:

Viewed as citizens they were a curious mixture. Our best man on the sub-machine guns was an eminent physician, sub-dean of a medical school.... The demonstration team for unarmed combat included a porter, a chauffeur, and an accountant. (The word combat was justified. They were so enthusiastic that there were days when our doctor-instructor did as much doctoring as instructing.) A pathologist surprisingly revealed as great a knowledge of the inside of grenades as of... humans.... My second-in-command at the school was a local civil servant who sat in an office... from nine

70. Holding-up the enemy – an 'invasion' scene in the City of London.

71. Home Guard and Canadian troops both take part in a street-fighting exercise.

to five every day. After five he came to life and developed nihilistic tendencies. I never hope to meet again a man who loved explosives more or could handle any type of grenade with greater ability. Legend had it that he slept with them under his pillow.

After the first few weeks, when ex-service recruits tried to teach their inexperienced comrades, most Home Guard training was provided within battalions by volunteers, who attended special weekend, or longer, courses for instructors. The first full-time Home Guard Training School was started in June 1940 at Osterley Park in Middlesex, by the public-spirited proprietor of *Picture Post*. In charge was a left-wing journalist who had fought in Spain, and his staff included three Spanish miners, whose talents were devoted, one observer noted, to 'de-bunking the tank' and teaching 'the use of Molotov-cocktails... and other un-cricket like methods of waging war'. Osterley was later taken over by the War Office, which founded several similar schools throughout the country. The best known was at Denby, code name — D, but there were several others — notably at Amberley, in Sussex, and at Burwash in the same county, the latter being run, like Osterley, by the author of a book on irregular warfare based on experience in Spain. One member of my company returned from Osterley having learned such useful arts as how to 'live off the country' by boiling potatoes in one's steel helmet.

To provide training for units on their home ground the War Office set up in February 1941 the first Travelling Wing, a team of half a dozen officers and NCOs under a former Marlborough College housemaster, who spent a week in an area providing intensive training every evening and on Saturday afternoon and Sunday. This proved so successful that eventually more than twenty were set up; a

72. Home Guards in a bombed area mop up 'enemy' snipers and strong points.

73. House-to-house fighting was practised in Britain's Blitzed streets by the Home Guard. Town Home Guard units scientifically studied the methods employed in Russia and Spain and the best means of combating the enemy's tactics.

street fighting school was also established in Birmingham, and there were soon several Battle Inoculation Schools, designed to accustom men to hearing the noise of bullets whistling over their heads and explosives going off only a few yards away. More peaceful were the summer camps under canvas, common by 1942, although owing to the 'forty-eight hours a month' limit on compulsory training, attendance was usually voluntary. Some ill-organised camps — where the food was, to quote one account, 'appalling and arrived hours late' — are still remembered with horror, but they provided the opportunity for officers and other ranks to get to know each other better. It was not until the Ministry of Food battalion's final camp in the summer of 1944, one member noted, that Army-style class-distinction really began to intrude, with the first-ever mess tent labelled 'Officers Only'.

After the tank-busting phase and — curiously enough — when the Home Guard was well equipped with weapons, came the unarmed combat phase. I was always sceptical of its value. My comrades and I *might* have stood up to an armed paratrooper charging at us with a rifle and bayonet by seizing the blade in our arms and smartly thrusting a leg out, so that he went flying over it, but personally I doubted whether this scene would have gone quite as scripted. Less orthodox methods of warfare, 'learnt at Osterley', felt one member of the 23rd Middlesex from Edgware, were 'so foreign to the British temperament that the value of the instruction was doubtful'. Lance-Corporal Ernest Raymond, a former clergyman, bravely conducted a one-man mutiny against one particularly savage instructor: 'I must suggest, sergeant,' he said in his best pulpit-style, 'that if we are only able to win the war by adopting all the things we have condemned in the Nazis, we may win it materially but they will have won it spiritually.'

74. A detachment of the Home Guard in a sandbagged emplacement in South London outskirts.

75. Home Guards rush a village under cover of a smoke bomb.

If rarely keen on drill, most Home Guards threw themselves eagerly into preparations to unmask the dreaded fifth-column. The 'Hawker' Platoon, in Surrey, convinced that their secret aircraft design documents would be an obvious target, at first gave up their lunch hour to training and in March 1941 began an evening parade each week, directly after working hours. The very first exercise was a spectacular success, for the attacking section employed 'a fifth-columnist' who 'donned blue overalls (over uniform), and peaked cap and put mud on [his] upper lip to resemble a moustache'. With this simple disguise, he was able to lob bricks, representing hand-grenades, at the opposing forces, and walk unchallenged into the objective. 'From that date, nowhere in Great Britain could there have been a… unit more fifth-column minded, and generally suspicious of all strangers in and out of uniform, clerical, monastic or otherwise.' In A. G. Street's village, soldiers billeted in the houses of the 'enemy' Home Guard proved useful as spies, and a street-fighting exercise was enlivened by a civilian 'fifth columnist' carrying a suitcase, from which at the vital moment he produced a tommy-gun, while one man who refused to join the Home Guard was 'shot' by the defenders by mistake — the only part of the whole scenario bearing much resemblance to reality. An official photographer at this time recorded a similar cautionary tale: a 'woman' wheeling a pram, having been allowed through a road block by a gullible Home Guard, hurls it on its side to provide cover and disposes of the defenders with a pistol, leaving the roadside as littered with corpses as the last scene in *Hamlet*. The BBC Home Guard was probably the only unit in the country able to call on professional actors within its ranks, and in one exercise two intruders successfully got past the barriers in Broadcasting House, London, with forged passes signed 'Adolf Hitler' and 'Stanley Baldwin'.

76. The Home Guard in action.

About many Home Guard activities there was by now a marked entertainment element, with inter-platoon competitions in bayonet fighting or musketry taking the place of village football or pub darts matches. In the village of Farningham, Kent where the second-in-command had in happier times been captain of the cricket club, a local resident who worked in the Foreign Office brought down a platoon of clerks and diplomats to provide the 'enemy' on a field day, like a visiting eleven. Most commanding officers encouraged such developments as helping to promote *esprit-de-corps,* that mysterious morale booster to which old-style soldiers often attached great importance. They were delighted when, in January 1941, regimental shoulder flashes began to be issued.

Full of regimental pride, according to its historian, was the 3rd County of London Home Guard which 'is apt to consider itself a "crack" battalion. It… has a habit peculiar, it is believed, to the …battalion — of wearing the numeral above the lettering in the identification badges carried on the sleeve. Its catchword is "Fighting Fulham" and its watchword: Retreat never, advance ever, victory is ours.'

Other units proud of their nicknames or titles were the 'Lincoln Imps' and the 'Highlands' platoon, to be found not in Scotland but manning the ramparts of Headington Hill and Magdalen Bridge as part of the 6th Oxfordshire (Oxford City) Battalion. The 43rd West Riding Battalion in Yorkshire even produced its own drinking song, which also has a flavour of self-mockery about it. It was sung to the tune of *Here's a Health unto His Majesty* and the 'Keates' and 'Frost' referred to were the Battalion CO and his 2 i/c, while 'Herr Schicklgruber' was, of course, Hitler:

77. Ruins and piles of rubble caused by German bombs add realism to these training exercises carried out by the London Home Guard.

Here's a Health unto the Forty-third:
With a fal la-la,
Confusion to the Axis herd,
With a fal... la.
With Keates and Frost we do not care
If Jerry comes by sea or air;
The Forty-third will comb their hair,
With a fal... la.
The Forty-third West Riding Batt.,
With a fal... la,
Will knock Herr Schiklgruber flat,
With a fal... la.
We'll take his paratroops for a ride,
We'll do our best to tan their hide,
And send them swimming back next tide,
With a fal... la.
The Forty-third's a damn fine crush,
With a fal... la.
We'll do our job without a fuss,
With a fal... la.
And when we've finished with the Boche,
We'll toast ourselves in gin and squash,
And when we're drunk we'll sing this tosh,
With a fal... la.

1940 had been a year of expedients. 1941 was a time of hard training, which intensified with the introduction of compulsion. Hitherto many men had tended to turn out only when they felt like it. Now proper training timetables and duty rosters could be worked out on the basis of 48 hours service a month, which

78. Learning how to shoot down aircraft with rifles.

79. RAF experts help the Home Guard with lectures on aircraft recognition.

80. Eliminating a sentry. Anti-invasion exercise, Worthing.

meant that most men attended a training parade each Sunday — which sometimes lasted the whole day — and did an all-night duty about one night in every eight. 1942, when compulsory service began, was felt by the historian of the Cambridgeshire battalions to be 'the flowering time for the Home Guard. Numbers were high, training had worked a remarkable transformation, weapons were now adequate to defence commitments and the spirit of the men was excellent.' Morale was never to be so high again, for by 1943 the need for the Home Guard was clearly past, with the Germans everywhere on the defensive and the British Isles, especially the Southern counties, choked with regular troops, including an increasing number of American combat divisions. Having built up the Home Guard, however, the government was not prepared to stand it down and instead constantly tried to find for it some new strategic role. In 1940 its task had been to observe and report; during 1941 the emphasis was on 'static defence', when, as a Devon battalion commander remembers, 'practically the whole system was based on a number of roadblocks with or without central "keeps".... We were told that the defence must be absolute and defenders must stand their ground.' This doctrine, however, made more appeal to the strategists than to the 'expendable' men on the ground. A member of the Wilmington platoon in Sussex was not enthusiastic when 'a big shot... came down one day to ginger us up' and having explained how 'the roadblocks and the tank traps... were to "contain" the Germans till the arrival of the real soldiers from the rear' ended encouragingly: 'Of course, probably none of you chaps will be alive when they get here and drive the Huns back into the sea.'

81. A Home Guard sniper in position.

82. Northern Command Home Guard counter-attack across a stream.

If dislodged from their strongpoints the Home Guard were expected to retreat to a small strongly defended area known as a 'keep', after the supposedly impregnable central tower in a medieval castle. Arrangements were complicated still further after September 1941 by the setting up of a civilian Invasion Committee in every town and village, to which the senior Guard officer was expected to belong, an unworkable arrangement in country areas as in Buckinghamshire:

> In one particular instance when 'parachute troops' had 'landed' in the neighbourhood of Loudwater and Woburn Green... the commander of the Flackwell Heath platoon... was discovered sitting with the Flackwelll Heath Invasion committee in a comfortable room enjoying the Sunday papers and a long glass of beer. The noise of battle could be plainly heard both at Woburn and Loudwater, but the Platoon Commander, although warned by an Umpire that the enemy would shortly overrun the village, insisted on obeying the orders of the Higher Command and remained with his beer.

Joint Home Guard and Civil Defence exercises were, one commander found, always liable to go wrong:

> One of the greatest headaches [wrote one junior officer] was that the Area Commanders were changed so often, and each one seemed to have a totally different conception of the Home Guard's proper role. One month we were static, next mobile, then back to static or betwixt and between, and it was very difficult to get some of the men to understand why, when they had been trained to do something somewhere, it was all scrapped and they were told that

83. Clearing an 'enemy' from a stronghold.

84. During a large scale 'invasion' of the City of London the evacuation of prisoners was practiced.

we should have to do something quite different somewhere else.

As the Home Guard grew stronger, plans for its use grew even more ambitious.

The Civil defence incidents were enacted... according to the timed schedule but the development of the military side of the exercise depended on the umpires.... Thus... a terrific street fighting battle in progress in the centre of a town [might be] interrupted by the police marching calmly down the High Street, halting at a road junction and roping it off, putting up a notice 'Bomb crater, traffic diverted'.... Respect for police authority is very deep seated. Both sides would obey the man in blue without question and go and fight in another street....

A Home Guard poet voiced the same complaint in *Punch*:

The brigadier we had last Spring
Said 'Static roles are not the thing;
As mobile as the midnight flea
Is what the Home Guard ought to be.'

Accordingly our 'schemes' were set
To make the Home Guard thirstier yet;
And all agreed that Brigadier
Must have some interest in beer.

He went; another came instead
Who deemed mobility was dead,
And thought the Home Guard, on the whole,
Far safer in a static role.

85. All over the country regulars co-operate in testing the Home Guard defenses. Here Canadian troops attack a Home Guard strongpoint.

86. Home Guard battle courses toughen their muscles to get them used to the fury and hazards of modern warfare.

We did not mind, Our Home Guard 'hut'
Is sited well for 'staying put'.
And one can usually sleep
Without disturbing all the sheep.

Besides some fresh and fertile brain
Is bound to change it all again.
And perch us, possibly, up trees —
Like monkeys and the Japanese.

No doubt some high strategic plan
Beyond the ken of common man
Dictates these changes in our job
From 'mob' to 'stat' and 'stat' to 'mob'.

Still it would help us all to know
More positively where to go,
In case, when Boches do appear,
We cannot find a brigadier.

If 1940 had been the great 'observation' period and 'roadblock' was the key-word in 1941 and 1942, by 1943 it had given way to 'the "ambush" period, when', to quote one battalion commander, '"get away" from roadblocks was permitted and even encouraged... local mobile reserves were prescribed and many roadblocks were derated to ambushes'. The fourth and final phase was more ambitious still. 'Passive defence fell into disrepute. Keeps or Defended Localities... were reduced in size... and permission was given by Higher Authority to

87. An assault course for Gloucester Home Guard.

88. London Transport Home Guard after clearing an enemy nest.

form a battalion Mobile Reserve... free to go on "fox hunting expeditions" to round up airborne or seaborne invaders.' This period was beginning when I joined the Home Guard; the Germans, we were told, were now expected to react to D Day by dropping whole brigades or even divisions, and our battalion was to join others to form a large counter-force. Like the mythical fifth-columnists of 1940 this was all complete nonsense, as British intelligence must have known. German hopes of disrupting the coming Second Front were pinned to the flying bomb; they had no troops to spare for marauding expeditions about the Sussex countryside.

My outstanding memory of the Home Guard at this period, like that of many others, is of Battle Drill, an attempt to break down elementary tactics into a series of simple movements and orders so that the soldier's responses on the battlefield became as automatic as on the parade ground. The standard 'right-flanking' or 'left-flanking' attack involved one party marching round to one side, turning left or right, hurling imaginary grenades and finally doubling forward — 'going in with the bayonet' — while another Section (to which I always did my best to belong) merely lay facing the enemy, shouting at the crucial moment: 'Cease covering fire!'

Inevitably, and fortunately, it is the occasions when training did not go according to 'the book' that are remembered best. The 'Demonstration Squad' of the 1st Berkshire Battalion, for example, were delighted when their officers 'searched a wood where they were hidden "à la Battle Drill" and could only find four out of eleven of us.... When half a dozen congregated under a tree for smoke after they had walked the wood two or three times one keen member of the Squad dropped an apple amongst them and said: "You're all dead." However, the officers refused to die and

89. Before. Regulars and Home Guards discuss the final details of an exercise.

90. After. A mug of tea and a smoke before the 'inquest' commences.

led Barney back to the rendezvous in triumph.' Exercises involving the Army presented special problems, for while the soldiers were usually only too happy to be 'killed' or 'captured' early on, Home Guards eliminated too soon were highly indignant and might even desert the battlefield. It was this difference to approach, rather than superior military skill, which so often led the Home Guard to enjoy gratifyingly easy victories when locked in combat with the Army. In Chatham the battalion adjutant realised during an attack on positions held by the Navy that 'something was obviously going wrong' as his men began 'bringing in large batches of smiling prisoners'. Interrogation revealed the reason: 'The Home Guard were using grenades of mutton cloth bags filled with whiting and it was just too much for the sailors to involve themselves in about three hours' kit cleaning.' Umpires in exercises involving the Ministry of Food battalion were faced with many problems. As its historian remarked: 'The "fog of war" is... even thicker on manoeuvres than actual fighting because the dead rise and argue and fight again, the wounded recover suddenly and... troops retire for a cup of coffee in the heat of battle.'

While the Army fought its mock battles over special training areas and 'ghost' villages, empty of civilians, the Home Guard had to carry out manoeuvres in built-up areas, often surrounded by mocking or hostile neighbours. The Birmingham battalion 'defending' Castle Bromwich aerodrome in April 1942 nearly became involved in a real battle for 'one of the members of the Allotment Holders' association at Brookvale that he had a complete row of onions pulled up and stolen during the night.... Although the allotment holder was duly compensated the incident aroused such a storm of abuse from the committee of the Allotment Holders' Club that they threatened if we set foot on the allotments again they would fight us a pitched battle with forks and spades.' For the BBC Home Guard it was peas, growing in the gardens outside its Glasgow premises as part of the 'Dig for Victory' campaign, which provided the trouble, for the management complained that men on guard were helping themselves. Their commander duly posed an admonitory notice which ended:

> I have repudiated this vile allegation against a fine body of men, and now... I think we should all stop eating the peas.

Before long every unit had its own story of an exercise that had gone wrong. One platoon in the 1st Berkshire Battalion, at Abingdon, never lived down its inability to 'understand a letter' of 'the dot-dash movement of a flag' during one communications exercise, for when 'the binoculars were brought into use... the "other station" proved to be a cow swishing its tail'. Another battalion claimed the rare distinction of having suffered an actual bombardment from Northover projectors, which their opponents in one exercise loaded with 'green apples as hard as stones' and 'small early potatoes'. A company taking part in a dockland defence exercise in the East End of London narrowly escaped a far worse fate, when, just in time, an umpire stopped one defender from pelting the attackers with his private invention, 'large rotten potatoes... pitted with scraps of old razor blades'. He was unmoved by suggestions that someone might have got hurt. 'You don't know 'em, mister. It 'ud just bounce off most of those b------s'.

Night exercises contained far worse hazards especially for those who were victims of 'blackout blindness'. The 'Hawker' Platoon contained a typical sufferer:

It was already dark when the platoon left Claremont with 'T' Section, led by Sgt D. in the van. Sgt D. took his men down the lawn on the west side of the house and was turning round to pass a message back to his second-in-command when suddenly his words were lost as without warning he stepped off the edge of the lawn into a small moat... a fall of some three to four feet.... Picking himself up, he proceeded. He had not gone another thirty yards, when he disappeared again — this time walking over the edge of the anti-tank ditch, a drop of nearly ten feet....

Bruised and shaken, but still determined, D. continued on his way... At this stage it was decided to put the sergeant in a rather more sheltered position and another Section took the lead... [but] contact was lost and 'T' Section were soon up to their knees in a stinking bog on the fringes of West End Common.... On they pushed until... D. sprawled over a fence of pointed chestnut palings and found himself on his face in the company of a colony of squealing piglets. Ultimately Horseshoe Clump was attacked and the exercise ended. The platoon formed up and began to march off with Sgt D. still game, giving a full account of his evening to the other Section Commanders as he limped along. But... in the middle of a sentence once more he disappeared, this time over the edge of a steep cutting through which the Portsmouth Road passes. Someone switched on a torch, and there was Sgt D. hanging for grim life to the protruding roots of a tree.

Even for those with good night vision, after-dark exercises could be appallingly difficult, though some men enjoyed the small-boy pleasures of 'blacking up' with burnt cork or cocoa to cover the tell-tale whiteness of face and hands. Really keen types even obscured their teeth, prompting the classic joke that 'Home Guards don't blacken their teeth; they take them out'.

At its best a major exercise could raise morale all round, like that in which the two Ministry of Food companies at Colwyn Bay played the part of 'airborne raiders':

Our third objective, at midnight, was the Post Office... Being warned of our approach, the defenders gave us a rough time... and the umpire called the affair off, a kindly enemy inviting us to their HQ for hot cocoa. Objective No. 4, Cromsville Garage... was taken by surprise but the defenders maintained we were under heavy Lewis gun fire for the last hundred yards. A tour of the defence layout by the umpires found the Lewis gun in question to be an imaginary one.... [on] to a beach defence post [where] the sentry was... 'nodding'.... It was found possible, therefore, for lieutenant H. and Sergeant S. to get through the wire and rush the post with Sten guns. 'What the hell?' exclaimed the surprised sergeant of the guard. 'Heil Hitler!' replied Lieutenant H.... At about 2 o'clock in the afternoon operations concluded. As we trooped home, tired, stiff, hungry and soaked in perspiration, the general feeling was one of satisfaction. We had pitted our strength and endurance against darkness, fatigue and physical obstacles... and emerged successful. It was a good feeling.

6
The Last Round

I was shot in the Battle of Blackberry Mountain,
Stabbed in a skirmish in Hafotty Lane,
Slaughtered in ambushes times beyond mention,
But always got up to be slaughtered again.

I died in a ditch to please Colonel Llewellyn,
I died on a mountain for Colonel Maclean;
I survived many battles that other men fell in,
I captured a gas works and drowned in a drain…

I remember occasions when sergeant said 'Blank you!'
(Occasions on which I prefer not to dwell).
So now we're dismissed and the King has said 'Thank you!',
I bid my ex-sergeant a Home Guard's farewell.

Member of the 11th Denbighshire Home Guard, 1944

From the beginning of 1944 the long decline of the Home Guard began; all but the most optimistic commanders began to acknowledge that they might never be needed after all. However the stalwart Colonel Crombie of Bideford, in his Special Order of the day welcoming 1944, assured his men that all chance of action was not yet lost:

> The United Nations are about to make the great assault and we know that the Beast, always dangerous at the best of times, will be particularly noxious in his dying paroxysms. This is when our Home Guard ordeal will come....
>
> Never, since the LDVs first fastened on their simple brassards and clutched their ridiculous bludgeons, has there been a time for relaxation; and assuredly that time is not yet.
>
> A conflict is about to be staged in comparison with which... Marathon... Austerlitz, Waterloo, Gettysburg, Passchendaele, even Stalingrad... will fade into insignificance... I give you... the motto for the Coming Year:
>
> NOW OR NEVER

It was in fact to be 'never'. But before this became apparent, a number of Home Guards had been in action against the Germans in anti-aircraft and coastal defence batteries. The first 'Ack Ack' Home Guards were volunteers, recruited in Aberdeen in April 1942, but before long batteries had to be kept up to strength by 'direction', from civilian life, or from ordinary battalions. The reaction of colliers of the Risca area to conscription into the 71st Monmouthshire Heavy Ack Ack Battery was, its historian admits, brief and pointed: 'Bloody pits of bloody Army man, not bloody both.' As for transfers from

91. & 92. The activities of the Home Guard was not restricted to the land. The Upper Thames Patrol, the 'navy' of the Home Guard, kept watch by day and night on the locks, towpaths, bridges and landing steps of London's riverside.

existing units, Home Guard commanders in the area regarded the artillery as a heaven-sent 'dumping ground' for persistent absentees and for the 'lame, halt and blind. Many of the men', this observer, considered, 'should not have been transferred at all', and the one local battalion commander who did loyally transfer 'almost a complete company of really effective — and trained — officers and men... was never afterwards forgiven for doing so, either by his battalion or his Home Guard superiors'.

Manning 4.5 or 3.7 inch guns in a heavy anti-aircraft battery was no job for the physically unfit, and after a time no-one over forty was accepted for it. Operating 'Z' batteries, firing lighter rockets from a simple projector, was less demanding. Here the age limit was sixty, and the rockets were always more attractive to recruits. The 101 (Durham) Rocket Battery, for example, which began recruiting in the spring of 1942 had, by September, its full complement of volunteers.

Within Anti-Aircraft Command the ill-feeling that so often existed between the Army and its part-time allies never occurred. No doubt the fact that the two were training and in action, side by side, helped, while by coming on duty one night in eight — raised in emergencies to one night in four — the Home Guard greatly eased the load on the full-time gunners. The Home Guard, in return were treated while on duty like ordinary soldiers, except that they did not get paid. Even among the reluctant recruits from the pits of Monmouthshire, one officer noticed, 'a few eyes brightened when it was explained that the manning teams would be fed, when operational duties were assumed. The mention of beer available in the NAAFI canteen won over even the most unenthusiastic, for beer was in very short supply at that time.'

93. Home Guard Marines practise landing at Lake Windermere.

94. Trent River Patrol finish a morning's work.

The Hyde Park rocket batteries had a particularly high reputation and, according to German prisoners, the Luftwaffe tried to give them a wide berth. The high standard of plotting was due to the Home Guards responsible being civilian scientists. The first 'kill' credited to a Home Guard Battery, however, was that of an enemy bomber which fell to No. 110 Battery on Tyneside. This had such an admirable effect that Battery Commanders subsequently had trouble preventing 'men not on duty from cluttering up the site' when the sirens sounded.

Although morale in Home Guard AA units was higher than in the rest of the force, the officers were even worse treated than those in ordinary units. The commander of a battery of 1400 to 1600 men, equal in size to an infantry battalion, was a major, not a lieutenant-colonel, and his second in command only a captain. The units suffered, too, from the usual reluctance of outside authority to accept that their military needs took precedence over civilian interests. The 101st AA Battery in Hyde Park found itself one Christmas turned out of its headquarters to provide the GPO with a temporary sorting office. A tree in a Royal Park was, it appeared, also sacrosanct, and as one observer wrote, 'the tree remains and the guns are grouped round it... out of alignment'. Although about 142,000 Home Guards served in Anti-Aircraft Batteries; 7000 others were assigned to coastal artillery.

About the value of two other sections of the Home Guard there can also be no question: 7000 members of the force were trained in Bomb Disposal, many of whom had to practise their skills in earnest. Although their courage was never put to the test, 5000 equally brave men were members of the 202nd and 203rd Battalions, which existed only on paper. These belonged

THE
SAME
OLD
STORY

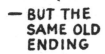

— BUT THE
SAME OLD
ENDING

95. For the 'mature' men of the Home Guard the call to arms was a handy cover story for going to the pub. From *Home Guard Humour*, 1944.

to the Auxiliary Units, six-man teams which, if the Germans had arrived, would in every sense have 'gone underground', moving into remote hideouts from which they would emerge, until caught, to create havoc behind the German lines. The auxiliary units were finally stood down on 19 November 1944, though because their existence was still secret they received no pubic thanks. The Auxiliary Units had no connection with the Home Guard Auxiliaries, consisting of female volunteers, oddly known at first as 'Nominated Women'. Even before the LDV had been set up, a few women had clamoured to be enrolled in an armed force and a few joined private organisations with names like the Amazon Defence League, and learned to shoot at their own expense. In the Summer of 1940 many women gave unofficial help in getting the LDV started, and some, even more unofficially, undertook unarmed mounted patrols of the countryside at dawn and dusk to relieve the burden on their hard-pressed menfolk.

Private efforts of this kind were obviously useful, but very different were suggestions that there should be a women's branch of the Home Guard. As the government pointed out, the Home Guard, unlike the regular Forces, did not need a permanent supporting army of cooks, drivers and telephonists while ample opportunities to help the war effort already existed in organisations like the Women's Voluntary Services. Pressure in Parliament for a female Home Guard began however in November 1940 though when, in June 1943, the first women Auxiliaries were recruited, only 4000 came forward, and fifteen months later, by stand-down, they numbered only 32,000. Unlike Civil Defence and the regular Forces the Home Guard remained, for all practical purposes, an all-male organisation.

Although nine out of ten Home Guards served as infantry in the

96. & 97. Mounted Home Guard in Berkshire and Devon.

General Service battalions, the force suffered from the first from a proliferation of 'fancy' units, which tended to attract attention out of all importance to their numbers. Many of the most unnecessary units, especially at the start, blossomed alongside rivers and lakes. There was one self-appointed Thames patrol, in the London suburbs, consisting of comfortably-off small boat owners, who sailed up and down the river in their own boats feeling they 'looked pretty smart in their monkey jackets, yachting caps and rubber boots'. They 'found the job they had allotted themselves quite exciting', though 'often when attempting to... board other craft the patrolling men were jeered at by bargees'. When offered a chance to join a regular, naval-organised service, from a base at Woolwich, of '120 members who had given their names at the [original] meeting only fourteen remained'.

In country districts the horse exercised a similar fascination and, until well on in the war, Mounted Patrols roamed Dartmoor, the South Downs, the Welsh Border, and other thinly populated areas, making a pretty picture as they leapt over hedges with all the dash of pre-1914 cavalry. Also to the world of publicity photographs rather than of real warfare belong the 'amphibious forces' which gallantly stormed ashore from pleasure boats in the Lake District and the Scottish lochs, and Assault Boats which charged up and down various canals. An Armoured train teamed up and down some northern railway line, for the Germans, it was assumed, would not be so unsporting as to blow up the track. To supplement normal methods of signalling there was even a Home Guard pigeon unit in Northamptonshire and a GPO Battalion in Cambridgeshire, recruited entirely from members of the Post Office. All the local Home Guard historian could find to say of this was that at least 'the Commanding Officer could not

98. A postmen group of Home Guard.

99. London Taxi Home Guard.

blame the lack of communications... so harassing to other Home Guard commanders'. Military transport, too, was not sufficient to content some commanders. There was in Sussex a Motor Bus Battalion and in London a mobile column of taxis. By happy chance 'the larger proprietors' all proved to have officer-like qualities and the ordinary cabbies to be qualified only as privates. They were consoled with the assurance that there 'should be no drills, no parades and no guards', a curious basis for any military unit, the driver's only commitment being to be available with his cab if required.

But a far greater wastage of manpower occurred in the 'private armies' of factory and office defence forces, many dating from 1940, when saboteurs were believed to lurk behind every pillar box. London Transport, for example, mustered no fewer than seven battalions, whose companies would have fought under such stirring banners as the 'Camberwell Tram Depot', the 'Bexley Heath Trolleybus Depot' and the 'Dartford Country Bus Garage'. The BBC, too, mobilised its own Home Guard. 'An orchestral rehearsal would be changed', wrote the historian of the BBC unit in Glasgow, 'and that meant no guard for three hours unless a press gang sweep on the clubroom proved fruitful....' In many factory units the members lived too far away to be available in an emergency and received no real training, being concerned solely to defend their own premises — even if the surrounding countryside was in enemy hands.

Although London Transport and the BBC, which were both obvious targets for enemy attack, retained their own Home Guard units to the end, from December 1940 onwards most of the smaller factory units were — not before time — merged into their local battalions. In Birmingham, for example, where Messrs

100. One of the mechanized sections of a southern county Home Guard battalion.

101. Sir Archibald Sinclair, Secretary of State for Air, inspects one of London's Home Guard 'flying squads'.

102. In Kent, motor-cycle signallers of the Home Guard receive last-minute instructions from the zone signals officer before setting out.

HP Sauce Ltd had, in June 1940, 'decided to form an LDV unit for the protection of the works' some members were later formed into 'a platoon with men from Norton Motors' for mobile duties, while 'the remainder of HP Sauce joined a contingent from Ansells' Brewery'.

But the real backbone of the Home Guard, from first to last, were the General Service battalions, the 'poor bloody infantry', and soon no march past in honour of *Aid to Russia Week* or *Wings for Victory Week* was complete without a detachment in battle dress; the anniversary of the Home Guard's foundation, on 14 May, was invariably made the occasion for some special ceremony. In May 1941 the Home Guard briefly took over the mounting of the guard at Buckingham Palace and, to its members, the King addressed a special message of thanks, which declared that 'The Home Guard stands in the direct line of the various bodies of Militia trained bands, Fencibles and Volunteers, the records of whose fine spirit and military aptitude adorn many a page of our history'. This was flattering, if untrue. A year later His Majesty became the Home Guard's colonel-in-chief and in 1943 the King took a salute at an anniversary parade in Hyde Park.

After D Day, in June 1944, it became increasingly clear that what the future held in store for the Home Guard was not battle honours but redundancy. Everywhere absenteeism increased, until it was announced that from 16 September no more men would be 'directed' into the Home Guard and attendance at parades would become voluntary. Despite many officers' boasts, the lifting of compulsion, in the words of one Northumberland company commander, 'knocked the bottom' out of the whole organisation. Even so, the warning to units, on 28 October, that the 'Stand Down' of the whole force, volunteers and all, was to begin on 1

103. Mechanized parades. On land. Home Guard Mechanized detachments ride past the saluting base where Lt. Gen. Sir Ronald Adam and the Lord Mayor of Sheffield take the salute.

104. A railwaymen group of Home Guard.

November was unexpected, especially in the still active Ack Ack Batteries. 'The surprising end to the activities of the Home Guard came as a tremendous disappointment to all in the Battery', wrote one officer. 'We had worked ourselves up to such a standard of enthusiasm, that the method of standing down acted rather like a very icy blast.' In contrast, too, to all the tributes paid to the Home Guard over the past four years, was the astonishing meanness with which it was treated now that it was no longer needed. Only after public protests did the government grudgingly agree that Home Guards could keep their boots and battledress — both valuable items at a time of clothes rationing. To older ex-servicemen it came as a disappointment, too, that no Home Guard medal was awarded, though those who had served for three years qualified for the Defence Medal. Men who had left earlier, often, like myself, to join the Forces, received nothing, not even a word of thanks or a certificate of service.

At the time compulsion ended, in September 1944, the Home Guard, excluding female Auxiliaries, numbered 1,727,095. (This compared to a strength of 400,000 around the end of May 1940, and a peak figure of 1,793,000 in March 1943.) The number of men who served for some months or years before resigning, reaching retiring age, or being called-up, was of course far larger and probably double this total. The cost to the nation, at least in money, of training this vast part-time Army was astonishingly small. Maintaining a fully-trained Home Guard, calculated one commander, cost the nation no more than one-fortieth the amount needed to support an ordinary solder even in peacetime, for the Home Guard received no pay and, when not on duty, fed, housed and clothed himself. The annual cost to the country for each Home Guard was estimated in 1944 at £9 5s (£9.25). The whole

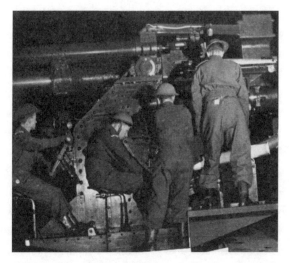

105. Home Guard relieve regular gunners for other spheres of operations.

106. Manning a naval coastal defense gun.

Home Guards total budget for a year was only £16,600,000, roughly equal to a single day's expenditure on the War. The Home Guard was an enormous bargain, the cheapest army of its size and firepower that any nation ever possessed.

Another record likely to remain unbroken is that the Home Guard suffered fewer casualties than any other comparable army. 1206 Home Guards were killed on duty, or died of wounds; 557 were injured, a total of 1763 — far fewer than one in every 1000 of those who served. Most of the casualties were caused by enemy action, particularly flying-bombs, which were of course also dangerous to all civilians. Where being a Home Guard *was* uniquely dangerous — more so than the regular Army — was in having to handle firearms and explosives with inadequate training. The worst single accident was probably the explosion of a No. 68 grenade, which always had an evil reputation when fired from a cup discharger, during a lecture in 1944, when six men were killed and fourteen hurt.

Heroism during such incidents accounted for many of the decorations awarded to Home Guards, which included thirteen George Medals and two George Crosses, both posthumous. One went to a sergeant killed rescuing people trapped after an air raid; the other to a 61-year-old lieutenant, who had survived two campaigns in South Africa and Flanders, only to lose his life when to protect his men, he threw himself on a Mills grenade which bounced back into the firing trench.

At last, on Sunday 3 December 1944, it was all over. There was an official march-past in Hyde Park before the King, which went off as well as such events always did, and smaller, local parades were held everywhere that damp and dismal Sunday. The Hampstead Home Guard made a characteristic exit. The officer in command

107. Oxford's Home Guard turn out for War Weapons Week.

of No. 15 Company, to which Ernest Raymond belonged, duly 'bellowed the command "Eyes *right*!" as we passed the mayors [of Hampstead and Hendon] but forgot for ever after to change it too "Eyes *front*!".... The Hampstead Home Guard marched... out of military into civil life with their eyes fixed permanently to the right.'

That day the King, as Colonel-in-Chief, issued a Special Army Order to the Home Guard, thanking them for their 'patient, ungrudging effort' and predicting — inaccurately it must be admitted — that: 'History will say that your share in the greatest of all our struggles for freedom was a vitally important one.' At 9 o'clock that evening he spoke to the nation over the radio. The Home Guard, which had begun with one broadcast, ended with another:

Over four years ago, in May 1940, our country was in mortal danger. The most powerful army the world had ever seen had forced its way to within a few miles of our coast. From day to day we were threatened with invasion.

For most of you — and I must add, for your wives too — your service in the Home Guard has not been easy. Some of you have stood for many hours on the gun sites, in desolate fields, or wind-swept beaches. Many of you, after a long and hard day's work, scarcely had time for food before you changed into uniform for the evening parade. Some of you had to bicycle for long distances to the drill hall or the rifle range....

But you have gained something for yourselves. You have discovered in yourselves new capabilities. You have found how men from all different kinds of homes and many different occupations can work together in a great cause, and how happy they can be

108. After the parade is over. Home Guard in an English pub.

109. The King honours the Home Guard. On the first anniversary of the Home Guard, 14 May 1941, at the King's desire, the Home Guard marched into Buckingham Palace to mount guard there for the first time.

with each other. I am very proud of what the Home Guard has done and I give my heartfelt thanks to you all.... I know that your country will not forget that service.

The Stand-Down of the Home Guard, which was finally completed on 31 December 1944, was not universally popular. Colonel Crombie of the 5th Devonshire issued what was to prove his final *Order of the Day* with evident reluctance:

It is true that we have not met Jerry in our Gate, but that was because he did not choose to present himself there.... Though Stood Down we shall not be quite *Out* as we may be recalled in an emergency to our old stations; and I am sure that in such an event, we shall be very glad to get once more into our armour....

But the call to action never came. A year later, in December 1945, the Home Guard was finally disbanded. Few of its members met again, and then only to take part in the Victory Parade through London, in June 1946, or to plan the regimental histories, which were soon appearing under such stirring titles as *Ever Faithful*; *Harrying the Hun*; *They Took Up Arms*; *Ploughshares into Swords*; *England Expected*; and just to ensure that the point was not overlooked: *The Lion Roared his Defiance, The Call Came and was Answered in Full*.

What contribution did the Home Guard make to victory? Apart from the real achievements already described, its usefulness, in my view, was greatest when the whole force was at its weakest. It did, in the summer of 1940, provide an outlet for the eager patriotism of many men, whose enthusiasm, once liberated, helped to inspire the whole country and to transform the national attitude to the

110. Civil Defence Services help to make the Home Guard anti-invasion exercises real tests of fighting conditions.

111. Learning to take messages.

112. A field kitchen.

war. The LDVs first duties, too, of observing and reporting, were useful and sensible; the real fighting then was to be left to the Army. Indeed the Home Guard could not have put up much of a fight as one ex-officer, who served in Devon 'from the first day to the last' later acknowledged:

> In those dusk and dawn watches on the fringe of Dartmoor, listening to those earliest of birds, the lark and cuckoo, bursting into song, even before the east began to lighten, possibly one man in each patrol was armed with anything at all. What could we have done if the coming day had suddenly spewed Huns from the skies — except run like hell, and even that would not have been good for some of our greybeards.... As a military force we were... a gigantic bluff.

Within a year or so it was different: on paper, at least, the Home Guard had now become a formidable force. But by then the need for it had passed, and by 1942, with Germany obviously on the defensive and the Home Guard's strength being maintained only by conscription, it was probably doing more harm than good. It tied up production that could have made life a little easier for the hard-pressed civilian, and deprived men now working flat-out for the war effort of precious sleep and recreation. As for the claim that the Home Guard provided a valuable training school for the Army, the truth was that the Army preferred to train all recruits from scratch, in its own way. The German army attached even less importance to it than the British. In the elaborate blueprints drawn up for *Operation Sealion* — the invasion of England — the Home Guard was simply ignored.

And yet, smile as one may at the excesses of its fire-eating commanders, begrudge as one may the millions of man-hours that might have been more profitably or pleasurably spent, there is about the Home Guard (especially in its early days) a touch of nobility as well as absurdity, that makes one almost proud to have belonged to it, and certainly proud to be a citizen of the country which created it. The reactions to being stood down of one Cornish Home Guard from the county's 11th Battalion, after serving right through the war, provide for the old Home Guard, if not for the one I knew, a fitting epitaph:

> Finally, as we take off our uniforms for the last time, we know we were needed... we 'was needed very sore'... I ... will end with the memory of a wild, bitter night deep in the winter of 1940-41. A crude, small shack crouched under a cliff hedge overlooking the Atlantic, six men on duty after a hard day's work; two on guard, four 'resting'. No bands, no pay, no medals, no glory. The sublime devotion to duty of it wrung my heart.

Sources

My main general source was Charles Graves, *The Home Guard of Britain* (Hutchinson, 1943) and I also drew on A. G. Street, *From Dusk to Dawn* (Harrap, 1943) and, by kind permission from Messrs Cassell, on Ernest Raymond, *Please You, Draw Near* (1969). On irregular warfare I consulted Tom Wintringham, *New Ways of War* (Penguin, 1940); John Brophy, *Home Guard Handbook* (Hodder & Stoughton, 1940); and John Langdon-Davies, *Parachutes over Britain* (Pilot Press, 1940). On the legal position of the Home Guard and the technical details of weapons I used a variety of authorities, and on the start of the LDV articles by ex-officers in various service magazines. On its later development, Simon Fine, *With the Home Guard* (1943), was helpful. My main source, however, was information and anecdotes in Home Guard regimental histories and magazines. Those I used most were Henry Smith, *Bureaucrats in Battledress, A History of the Ministry of Food Home Guard* (n.d.); D. C. Crombie, *History of the 5th*

(Bideford) Battalion, Devon Home Guard (1946); *The Choughs Annual Register* (11th Cornwall [Newquay] Battalion) (n.d.); *We Also Served. The Story of the Home Guard in Cambridgeshire* (1944); H. E. Flight (editor), *North West (London) Frontier, No. 6 Company, 23rd Middlesex Battalion* (1946); E. D. Barclay, *History of the 45th Warwickshire (Birmingham) Home Guard* (1945); G. D. C. Garrett, *The Hawker Platoon, 'E' Company, 53rd Surrey Battalion* (n.d.); L. W. Kentish, *Home Guard, Bux 4. Records and Reminiscences of the 4th Buckinghamshire Battalion* (n.d.); *The Story of the First Berkshire Battalion (Abingdon) Home Guard by Ourselves* (1945); H. Holloway and H. Banks (editors), *The Northamptonshire Home Guard* (1949); L. A. Mohan, *Historical Sketch, 71 Monmouth Home Guard H.A.A. Battery* (1944); *The Watch on the Braids. The Record of an Edinburgh Home Guard Company 1940-1944* (1944).

As almost all the above were privately printed and circulated it has rarely proved possible to trace the copyright-owners, to whom graceful acknowledgement is made and appropriate apologies offered.

List of Illustrations

12. Home Guard train in the correct use of the bayonet. © Jonathan Reeve JR1656b87p27T 19391945.

13. LDV practise shooting down German parachutist using a teddy bear. © Jonathan Reeve JR1662b87p33TL 19391945.

14. Home Guards were often first on the scene when enemy aircraft crashed. © Jonathan Reeve.

15. An evening route march takes the local Home Guard unit through the village high street. © Jonathan Reeve JR1592b80p21B 19391945.

16. Local Defence Volunteers prepare for the real thing. LDV practice erecting temporary barricades against invading German troops. © Jonathan Reeve JR1593b83p258T 19391945.

17. Improvised transport! From *Home Guard Humour*, 1944. © J & C McCutcheon Collection.

18. This tower, on the estate of Lord Hastings, has once again come into its own. Used during five previous threats of invasion, it serves today as a Home Guard observation post © Jonathan Reeve JR1704b87p79 19391945.

19. Home Guard – miners in South Wales. © Jonathan Reeve JR1687b87p57 19391945.

20. Home Guard at the Houses of Parliament. © Jonathan Reeve JR1686b87p56 19391945.

21. London Home Guard in a public display involving the much cartooned pike. © Jonathan Reeve JR1657b87p27B 19391945.

22. Testing the defences of an airfield, Southern Command. © Jonathan Reeve JR1690b87p61B 19391945.

23. Home Guard on parade, Springfield in Essex. © Jonathan Reeve JR1652b87p23 19391945.

24. A Home Guard firing through a smoke screen. © Jonathan Reeve JRbp 19391945.

25. In Kent, Major Holdness and his two sons overhaul their equipment. © Jonathan Reeve JR1641b87p13T 19391945.

26. In South Wales Sgt Bill Davies, a miner, sets out to mount guard. © Jonathan Reeve JR1642b87p13B 19391945.

27. Some of the duties assigned to Home Guardsmen were not appreciated. From *Home Guard Humour*, 1944. © J & C McCutcheon Collection.

28. Winston Churchill, who created the Home Guard, wielding a Thompson machine gun. © Amberley Archive.

29. Local Defence Volunteers. © Jonathan Reeve JR1613b81p47 19391945.

30. & 31. *Top:* LDV volunteers are taught how to throw 'Molotov

Cocktails' a practical means of dealing with tanks. *Below:* The effect of one of these 'cocktails' on a dummy tank towed by a car. The bombs, which are bottles partially filled with a mixture of petrol, paraffin and crude oil, were used with much success during the Finnish campaign. © Jonathan Reeve JR1594b83p258B 19391945 and © Jonathan Reeve JR1595b83p259 19391945.

32. American Independence Day. A march past of the American Squadron of the Home Guard. © Jonathan Reeve JR1705b87p80 19391945.

33. After Dunkirk the village barber carried on during periods of guard duty. © Jonathan Reeve JR1703b87p77T 19391945.

34. Many of the running jokes in the BBC TV series Dad's Army were not new. From *Home Guard Humour*, 1944. © J & C McCutcheon Collection.

35. Numerous pamphlets and instruction books were published during the war feeding a seemingly insatiable appetite for guidance on how to repel a potential German invasion. © Amberley Archive.

36, 37, 38, & 39. Firing a rifle, from a Home Guard manual. © Amberley Archive.

40. Firing a rifle from behind cover, standing, from a Home Guard manual. © Amberley Archive.

41. Diagram of an observation post from a Home Guard manual. © Amberley Archive.

42. A concealed sniper position from a Home Guard manual. © Amberley Archive.

43. Along the cliff edge winds a unit of Home Guard to their posts. © Jonathan Reeve JR1604b82p136-7 19391945.

44. Home Guard on patrol in the city. © Jonathan Reeve JR1643b87p14 19391945.

45. Home Guard unit on a tactical exercise on one of England's beaches in preparation for any attack. © Jonathan Reeve JR1598b83p262 19391945.

46. Armed Home Guard patrolling a railway line. © Jonathan Reeve JR1596b83p260 19391945.

47. Home Guards prepare to deal with an 'invader' by means of Molotov cocktails. © Jonathan Reeve JR1606b82p138B 19391945.

48. Regular instructors instruct Home Guardsmen in the use of the 'sticky' bomb and other up-to-date anti-tank devices. © Jonathan Reeve JR1661b87p31B 19391945.

49. A 'sticky bomb'. © Amberley Archive.

50. The comic possibilities of the 'sticky bomb' from *Home Guard Humour*, 1944. © J & C McCutcheon Collection.

51. & 52. Grenade throwing needs practice, (top) whether as here with the 36M grenade or (below) with Molotov cocktails. © Jonathan Reeve JR1658b87p29T 19391945 and © Jonathan Reeve JR1659b87p29B 19391945.

53. A farmer from Oxfordshire getting ready for a parade. © Jonathan Reeve JR1640b87p12 19391945.

54. & 55. (top) Webley pistol .45 inch or .38 inch and (below) diagram showing the parts of government issue rifle from a Home Guard manual. © Amberley Archive.

56. & 57. Home Guards are instructed in the use of the Lewis machine gun (top). The Lewis light machine gun from a Home Guard manual. © Jonathan Reeve JR1591b80p21T 19391945 and © Amberley Archive

58. & 59. (top) The Bren light machine gun, (below) the Thompson sub-machine gun .45 inch from a Home Guard manual. © Amberley Archive. © Amberley Archive.

60. Home Guardsmen learning how to use new automatic machine guns. © Jonathan Reeve JR1676b87p45 19391945.

61. An instructor demonstrates how to use the 'cup discharger' for grenades. © Jonathan Reeve JR1673b87p43T 19391945.

62. Home Guard armoured cars on patrol in the North of Scotland. © Jonathan Reeve JR1670b87p39B 19391945.

63. This Rolls Royce monster, donated to the Home Guard, was converted by the men themselves. © Jonathan Reeve JR1669b87p39T 19391945.

64. Cumberland Home Guard tensed for the word 'fire' behind a Spigot Mortar, one of the Home Guards' formidable pieces of sub-artillery. © Jonathan Reeve JR1678b87p47 19391945.

65. On the anniversary of the birth of the Home Guard, demonstration teams fire the Northover Projector in the heart of London. © Jonathan Reeve JR1677b87p46 19391945.

66. Brigadier General J.V. Campbell, VC, who commanded a Gloucestershire battalion, inspects the new issue of sten guns. © Jonathan Reeve JR1675b87p44 19391945.

67. Diagram showing a typical tank ambush from a Home Guard manual. © Amberley Archive.

68. Use of explosive to sabotage railways from a Home Guard manual. © Amberley Archive.

69. Home Guard in training. © Jonathan Reeve JR1601b82p134 19391945.

70. Holding-up the enemy – an 'invasion' scene in the City of London. © Jonathan Reeve JR1603b82p135B 19391945.

71. Home Guard and Canadian troops both take part in a street-fighting

exercise. © Jonathan Reeve JR1602b82p135T 19391945.

72. Home Guards in a bombed area mop up 'enemy' snipers and strong points. © Jonathan Reeve JR1605b82p138T 19391945.

73. House-to-house fighting was practised in Britain's Blitzed streets by the Home Guard. Town Home Guard units scientifically studied the methods employed in Russia and Spain and the best means of combating the enemy's tactics. © Jonathan Reeve JR1617b81p56-7 19391945.

74. A detachment of the Home Guard in a sandbagged emplacement in South London outskirts. © Jonathan Reeve JR1599b83p299T 19391945.

75. Home Guards rush a village under cover of a smoke bomb. © Jonathan Reeve JR1607b82p139B 19391945.

76. The Home Guard in action. © Jonathan Reeve JR1609b82p17 19391945.

77. Ruins and piles of rubble caused by German bombs add realism to these training exercises carried out by the London Home Guard. © Jonathan Reeve JR1611b81p44 19391945.

78. Learning how to shoot down aircraft with rifles. © Jonathan Reeve JR1663b87p33TR 19391945.

79. RAF experts help the Home Guard with lectures on aircraft recognition. © Jonathan Reeve JR1664b87p33B 19391945.

80. Eliminating a sentry. Anti-invasion exercise, Worthing. © Jonathan Reeve JR1689b87p61T 19391945.

81. A Home Guard sniper in position. © Jonathan Reeve JR1666b87p35B 19391945.

82. Northern Command Home Guard counter-attack across a stream. © Jonathan Reeve JR1690b87p63T 19391945.

83. Clearing an 'enemy' from a stronghold. © Jonathan Reeve JR1691b87p63B 19391945.

84. During a large scale 'invasion' of the City of London the evacuation of prisoners was practiced. © Jonathan Reeve JR1692b87p65T 19391945.

85. All over the country regulars co-operate in testing the Home Guard defenses. Here Canadian troops attack a Home Guard strongpoint. © Jonathan Reeve JR1693b87p65B 19391945.

86. Home Guard battle courses toughen their muscles to get them used to the fury and hazards of modern warfare. © Jonathan Reeve JR1694b87p66 19391945.

87. An assault course for Gloucester Home Guard. © Jonathan Reeve JR1695b87p67T 19391945.

88. London Transport Home Guard after clearing an enemy nest. © Jonathan Reeve JR1696b87p67B 19391945.

89. Before. Regulars and Home Guards discuss the final details of an exercise. © Jonathan Reeve JR1697b87p69T 19391945.

90. After. A mug of tea and a smoke before the 'inquest' commences. © Jonathan Reeve JR1698b87p69B 19391945.

91. & 92. The activities of the Home Guard was not restricted to the land. The Upper Thames Patrol, the 'navy' of the Home Guard, kept watch by day and night on the locks, towpaths, bridges and landing steps of London's riverside. © Jonathan Reeve JR1597b83p261 19391945 and © Jonathan Reeve JR1683b87p51B 19391945.

93. Home Guard Marines practise landing at Lake Windermere. © Jonathan Reeve JR1653b87p24T 19391945.

94. Trent River Patrol finish a morning's work. © Jonathan Reeve JR1654b87p24B 19391945.

95. For the 'mature' men of the Home Guard the call to arms was a handy cover story for going to the pub. From *Home Guard Humour*, 1944. © J & C McCutcheon Collection.

96. & 97. Mounted Home Guard in Berkshire and Devon. © Jonathan Reeve JR1647b87p19T 19391945, © Jonathan Reeve JR1648b87p19B 19391945.

98. A postmen group of Home Guard. © Jonathan Reeve JR1650b87p21T 19391945.

99. London Taxi Home Guard. © Jonathan Reeve JR1649b87p20 19391945.

100. One of the mechanized sections of a southern county Home Guard battalion. © Jonathan Reeve JR1667b87p37T 19391945.

101. Sir Archibald Sinclair, Secretary of State for Air, inspects one of London's Home Guard 'flying squads'. © Jonathan Reeve JR1668b87p37B 19391945.

102. In Kent, motor-cycle signallers of the Home Guard receive last-minute instructions from the zone signals officer before setting out. © Jonathan Reeve JR1672b87p41 19391945.

103. Mechanized parades. On land. Home Guard Mechanized detachments ride past the saluting base where Lt. Gen. Sir Ronald Adam and the Lord Mayor of Sheffield take the salute. © Jonathan Reeve JR1682b87p51T 19391945.

104. A railwaymen group of Home Guard. © Jonathan Reeve JR1651b87p21B 19391945.

105. Home Guard relieve regular gunners for other spheres of operations. © Jonathan Reeve JR1679b87p49T 19391945.

106. Manning a naval coastal defense gun. © Jonathan Reeve JR1680b87p49B 19391945.

107. Oxford's Home Guard turn out for War Weapons Week. © Jonathan Reeve JR1681b87p50 19391945.

108. After the parade is over. Home Guard in an English pub. © Jonathan Reeve JR1699b87p71 19391945.

109. The King honours the Home Guard. On the first anniversary of the Home Guard, 14 May 1941, at the King's desire, the Home Guard marched into Buckingham Palace to mount guard there for the first time. © Jonathan Reeve JR1684b87p53 19391945.

110. Civil Defence Services help to make the Home Guard anti-invasion exercises real tests of fighting conditions. © Jonathan Reeve JR1700b87p73 19391945.

111. Learning to take messages. © Jonathan Reeve JR1701b87p75T 19391945.

112. A field kitchen. © Jonathan Reeve JR1702b87p75B 19391945.

Colour Section

Plate 1. Official War Artist Eric Kennington travelled the length and breadth of Britain during 1942-3 to capture the essence of spirit of the Home Guard. Here is his portrait of Corporal Robertson, City of Edinburgh Home Guard. Portrait by Eric Kennington. Photo © Jonathan Reeve JR1708b88fp24 19391945.

Plate 2. Anti-aircraft gunners, London Home Guard. Eric Kennington. Photo © Jonathan Reeve JR1709b88fp25 19391945.

Plate 3. Sergeant Bluett, Cornwall Home Guard. Photo © Jonathan Reeve JR1706b8fp9 19391945.

Plate 4. LDV River Severn Patrol. © Jonathan Reeve JR1655b87p25 19391945.

Plate 5. Firing a rifle from behind cover, kneeling and lying, from a Home Guard manual. © Amberley Archive.

Plate 6. The Home Guard was truly a mass organization and spawned a mini publishing industry, this is the cover of a 1944 'toilet' book, *Home Guard Humour*. © J & C McCutcheon Collection.

Plate 7. The Home Guard was truly a mass organization and spawned a mini publishing industry, this is the cover of a 1944 memoir, *With the Home Guard* by Home Guardsman Captain Simon Fine. © Jonathan Reeve JR1632b87pfc 19391945.

Plate 8. Cover of one of the many Home Guard manuals produced during the war. © Amberley Archive.

Plate 9. Battery Sergeant-Major Dawson, Yorkshire Home Guard. Portrait by Eric Kennington. Photo © Jonathan Reeve JR1707b88fp17 19391945.

Plate 10. Home Guard training. © Jonathan Reeve JR1608b82p152 19391945.

Plate 11. An instructor demonstrates how to use the 'cup discharger'. A platoon commander uses one. © Jonathan Reeve JR1674b87p43B 19391945.

Plate 12. A Home Guard sniper in camouflage. © Jonathan Reeve JR1665b87p35T 19391945.

Plate 13. Coast Defense Gunners, Lancashire Home Guard. Portrait by Eric Kennington. Photo © Jonathan Reeve JR1710b88fp32 19391945.

Plate 14. Sergeant Hampshire, Middlesex Home Guard. Portrait by Eric Kennington. Photo © Jonathan Reeve JR1712b88fp44 19391945.

Plate 15. Company Sergeant-Major Waters, Lancashire Home Guard. Portrait by Eric Kennington. Photo © Jonathan Reeve JR1711b88fp41 19391945.

Plate 16. Coast Defence searchlight, Lancashire Home Guard. Eric Kennington. Photo © Jonathan Reeve JR1713b88fp45 19391945.

Plate 17. 'They don't like it up "em"' . Home Guard Corporal Charles Batchelor could have said. © Jonathan Reeve JR1688b87p59 19391945.

Also available from Amberley Publishing

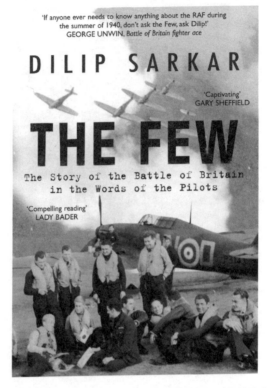

'If anyone ever needs to know anything about the RAF during the summer of 1940, don't ask the Few, ask Dilip!'
GEORGE UNWIN, *Battle of Britain fighter ace*

DILIP SARKAR

'Captivating'
GARY SHEFFIELD

THE FEW

The Story of the Battle of Britain in the Words of the Pilots

'Compelling reading'
LADY BADER

The history of the Battle of Britain in the words of the pilots

'Over the last 30 years Dilip Sarkar has sought out and interviewed or corresponded with numerous survivors worldwide. Many of these were not famous combatants, but those who formed the unsung backbone of Fighter Command in 1940. Without Dilip's patient recording and collation of their memories, these survivors would not have left behind a permanent record.' LADY BADER
'A well-researched detailed chronicle of the Battle of Britain'. HUGH SEBAG MONTEFIORE

£14.99 Paperback
129 photographs
320 pages
978-1-4456-0050-5

Available from all good bookshops or to order direct
Please call **01453-847-800**
www.amberleybooks.com

Also available from Amberley Publishing

How to fly the legendary fighter plane in combat using the manuals and instructions supplied by the RAF during the Second World War

'A Must' *INTERCOM: THE AIRCREW ASSOCIATION*

An amazing array of leaflets, books and manuals were issued by the War Office during the Second World War to aid pilots in flying the Supermarine Spitfire, here for the first time they are collated into a single book with the original 1940s setting. An introduction is supplied by expert aviation historian Dilip Sarkar. Other sections include aircraft recognition, how to act as an RAF officer, bailing out etc.

£9.99 Paperback
40 illustrations
264 pages
978-1-84868-436-2

Available from all good bookshops or to order direct
Please call **01453-847-800**
www.amberleybooks.com

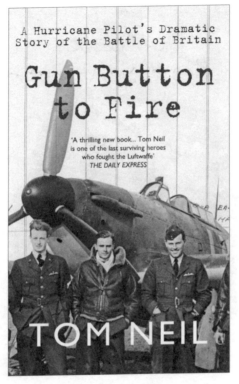

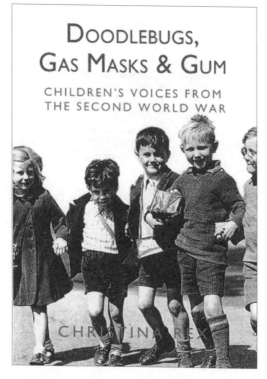

Also available from Amberley Publishing

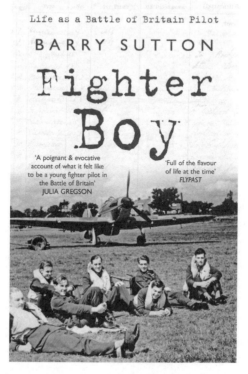

The Battle of Britain memoir of Hurricane pilot Barry Sutton, DFC

'A refreshing book written just after the events' *INTERCOM: THE AIRCREW ASSOCIATION*

'The reader will find in Squadron Leader Sutton the virtues which the country has come to admire in the RAF flier – courage, determination, persistence, unfailing good humour, optimism, faith' *THE TIMES*

At 23 years of age, Barry Sutton had experienced more than the average person experiences in a lifetime. This book, based on a diary he kept during the war, covers September 1939 to September 1940 when he was shot down and badly burned.

£10.99 Paperback
61 illustrations
192 pages
978-1-4456-0627-9

Available from all good bookshops or to order direct
Please call **01453-847-800**
www.amberleybooks.com

Also available from Amberley Publishing

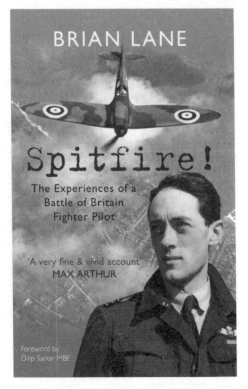

The remarkable Battle of Britain experiences of Spitfire pilot
Brian Lane, DFC

'A very fine and vivid account' MAX ARTHUR

Brian Lane was only 23 when he wrote his dramatic account of life as a Spitfire pilot during the Battle
of Britain in the summer of 1940. Lane was an 'ace' with six enemy 'kills' to his credit and was awarded
the DFC for bravery in combat. The text is honest and vibrant, and has the immediacy of a book
written close the event, untouched, therefore, by the doubts and debates of later years.

£9.99 Paperback
65 illustrations
160 pages
978-1-84868-354-9

Available from all good bookshops or to order direct
Please call **01453-847-800**
www.amberleybooks.com

Also available from Amberley Publishing

A fabulous slice of wartime nostalgia, a facsimile edition of the manual used by the Land Girls during the Second World War

'Fascinating... gives a good insight into the history of he WLA'
BBC WHO DO YOU THINK YOU ARE MAGAZINE

First published in 1941, *Land Girl* was a practical guide for the city slickers who were recruited into the Women's Land Army and sent to work on farms in the English countryside to replace the men who had joined up. An amazing period piece, hundreds of thousands of copies were printed and sold and it became one of the year's best-selling books.

£9.99 Paperback
25 illustrations
160 pages
978-1-4456-0279-0

Available from all good bookshops or to order direct
Please call **01453-847-800**
www.amberleybooks.com

Also available from Amberley Publishing

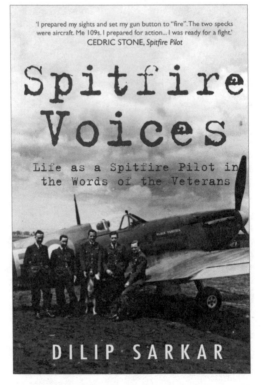

'I prepared my sights and set my gun button to "fire". The two specks
were aircraft. Me 109s. I prepared for action... I was ready for a fight.'
CEDRIC STONE, *Spitfire Pilot*

Spitfire
Voices

Life as a Spitfire Pilot in
the Words of the Veterans

DILIP SARKAR

*Spitfire fighter pilots tell their extraordinary stories of combat
during the Second World War*

'I prepared my sights and set my gun button to "fire". The two specks were aircraft. Me 109s. I prepared
for action... I was ready for a fight.' CEDRIC STONE, Spitfire Pilot

'There is nothing glamorous in being a fighter pilot. There is nothing glamorous in killing and being
killed. Exciting, very exciting, sometimes too exciting, but definitely not glamorous, not even in a
Spitfire.' MAURICE MACEY, Spitfire Pilot

£20 Hardback
169 Photographs
360 pages
978-1-4456-0042-0

Available from all good bookshops or to order direct
Please call **01453-847-800**
www.amberleybooks.com

Also available from Amberley Publishing

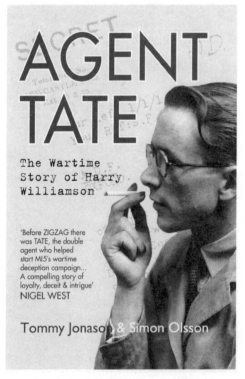

The wartime career of British double-cross agent TATE, who makes agent ZIGZAG look like a bit of a wuss...

'Before ZIGZAG there was TATE, the double agent who helped start MI5 s wartime deception campaign. A compelling story of loyalty, deceit and intrigue' NIGEL WEST

This is the Second World War career of the longest serving double agent in the Double Cross system, Harry Williamson. Harry operated from September 1940 to the end of war after initially being parachuted into England by the Nazi secret service, the Abwehr. After the war he settled in Watford and worked as a photographer. He was almost completely anonymous (although still protected by MI5), partly through fear of revenge, until his name was revealed in the 1990s.

£20 Hardback
56 illustrations
272 pages
978-1-4456-0481-7

Also available from Amberley Publishing

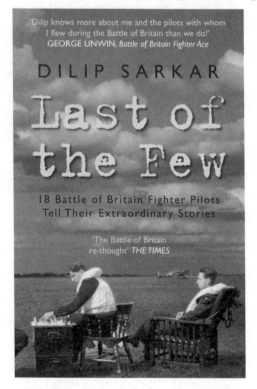

18 Spitfire and Hurricane fighter pilots recount their experiences of combat during the Battle of Britain

£9.99 Paperback
55 Photographs
224 pages
978-1-4456-0282-0

Also available from Amberley Publishing

A fabulous slice of wartime nostalgia, a facsimile edition of the propaganda booklet issued following victory in the Battle of Britain

Also available from Amberley Publishing

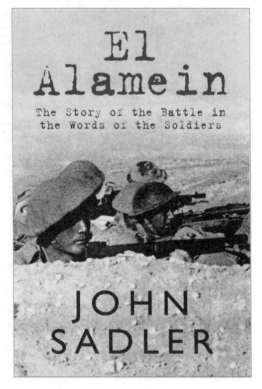

This is the story of El Alamein and the British soldiers who fought in it

'There was for me no excitement in the charge. I'd seen it all before, and after a certain time you look round the faces of your mates and you realize with a shock how few of the original mob are left. Then you know it's only a matter of time before you get yours. All I wanted to do was to get across that bloody ground and through the guns.' *BRITISH INFANTRYMAN*

The epic battle in Egypt between the Axis forces led by Rommel 'the Desert Fox' and Britain's 'Desert Rats' in the words of the soldiers themselves.

£12.99 Paperback
70 illustrations
288 pages
978-1-4456-0626-2

Available from all good bookshops or to order direct
Please call **01453-847-800**
www.amberleybooks.com

An extraordinary true
story of combat in the
Battle of Britain

SPITFIRE
PILOT
ROGER HALL, DFC

The intensely evocative memoir of one of 'the Few',
Spitfire pilot Roger Hall

The Battle of Britain memoir of Roger Hall, a Spitfire pilot in 152 Squadron based in the South East of England, the heart of the fighting during the epic battle. Roger recounts in exhaustive detail his own experience of air-to-air combat with Me109s and Me110s (he shot down three enemy aircraft during the Battle of Britain), and that of his fellow pilots. Hall had no compunction in revealing his fear of wartime flying. He strips away the veneer of glory, smart uniforms and wild parties and uncovers the ordinary, very human young men who lived a life in which there was no tomorrow. There is no nostalgia here.

£20 Hardback
50 photographs
224 pages
978-1-4456-0557-9

Available January 2012 from all good bookshops or to order direct
Please call **01453-847-800**
www.amberleybooks.com

Also available from Amberley Publishing

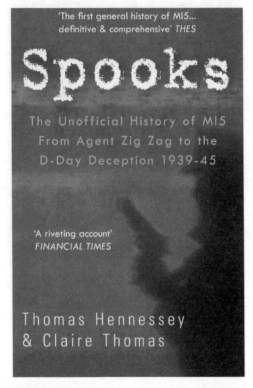

'The first general history of MI5...
definitive & comprehensive' *THES*

Spooks

The Unofficial History of MI5
From Agent Zig Zag to the
D-Day Deception 1939-45

'A riveting account'
FINANCIAL TIMES

Thomas Hennessey
& Claire Thomas

The history of MI5 during the Second World War

During the Second World War, the Security Service, through brilliant officers such as Guy Liddell, Dick White and the fearsome spy-breaker, 'Tin-eye' Stephens, commandant of MI5's interrogation centre, Camp 020, successfully ran the Double Cross (XX) system. XX agents such as the dynamic, womanising petty criminal ZIGZAG, the suave TRICYCLE and the aptly named CARELESS laid the basis for Operation FORTITUDE in which MI5's agents BRUTUS and GARBO were central to the success of the greatest deception in modern military history: convincing Hitler that the D-Day landings in Normandy were an elaborate diversion to the 'real' Allied landings at Calais. It was MI5's finest hour.

£12.99 Paperback
512 pages
978-1-4456-0184-7

Available from all good bookshops or to order direct
Please call **01453-847-800**
www.amberleybooks.com

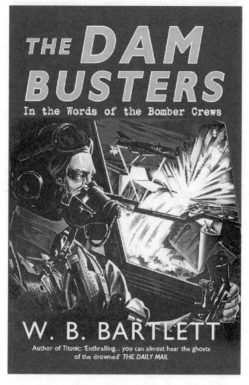

Also available from Amberley Publishing

Dad's Army by the men who were there –
profusely illustrated with cartoons

In May 1945, as the Home Guard stood down, an enterprising small publisher in Birmingham produced
Home Guard Humour – a lighthearted look at the five-year history of the Home Guard. Within the
pages of the booklet are contained all of the standard 'Dad's Army'-style jokes and one wonders if it was
this booklet which encouraged the writing of one of Britain's most loved sit-coms.

£4.99 Paperback
30 illustrations
32 pages
978-1-4456-0186-1

Available from all good bookshops or to order direct
Please call **01453-847-800**
www.amberleybooks.com

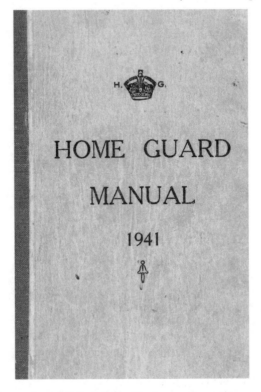

Index

Author's
Acknowledgements

My thanks are due to all those who supplied me with information, including contributors to my *How We Lived Then* and Mr H. de Beaufort-Saunders. I acknowledge the help of the staff of the Imperial War Museum, especially Mr Christopher Frayling, who kindly 'vetted' the chapter on weapons; also of Miss Idina Le Geyt, who did much of the factual research; of Miss Christine Vincent, and of my secretary, Miss Stephanie Tooms. The book was inevitably produced under some pressure and it was pleasant to find that all those involved displayed what might be called 'the Home Guard spirit'.

N.R.L.
(Ex-Private, 'F' Company, 3rd Sussex (Horsham) Battalion, Home Guard.)